The Power
of Insight

The Power of Insight

Finding the Courage to Connect® in Business

INGRID SPRONCK
THOMAS J. BEEREPOOT

PARAVIEW
Special Editions

New York

Cover photo by Erik Schilt Eye-Eye Fotografie
Cover design by smythtype

ISBN: 1-931044-62-7

Library of Congress Catalog Number: 2003107974

Contents

Preface / 7

CHAPTER 1: An Introduction to Insight / 12

CHAPTER 2: Connecting and Overcoming Reason
and Emotion / 27

CHAPTER 3: Connecting, Overcoming, and Seeing / 46

CHAPTER 4: Discomfort: Breaking Through the Barriers / 64

CHAPTER 5: Accelerating Success: Doing Things Differently / 86

CHAPTER 6: The Courage to Overcome in Business / 93

Frequently Asked Questions / 104

Summary / 109

Afterword: The Future / 113

Preface

U nexpected setbacks, cost reductions, innovations, rapid market change, the need for improved customer service, and concerns about the environment, safety, discrimination, and poverty indicate that it might be time for leaders to take a different approach — maybe even a revolutionary approach — to the increased pressures, demands, and changes in our workplace.

This book provides such an approach. *The Power of Insight* is about the power of what we call "seeing." Seeing is that snap-your-finger moment, the "aha" moment when we "get it," "see it," and know precisely what to do. This flash of insight and breakthrough thinking occurs when reason and emotions are connected and over-come, allowing us to see things in an entirely new light. Those who best see reality can make the best decisions. And only by seeing and going beyond differences can leaders lead well.

Past

Fifteen years ago, when I (Ingrid) was working as an independent management consultant, one of my clients asked me to work with Frank, a manager who was no longer performing well in his job. The client told me that if my coaching didn't work, he would have no choice but to let Frank go.

At our first session, Frank brought along his four-month-old daughter. Having lost my father at a very early age, I found myself identifying with this little girl. I could not bear the thought that she would suffer if her father lost his job.

During the nights following this first session, I could not sleep. How could I help the little girl and her father? How could I help Frank move out of his state of apathy?

During this time, I developed the Courage to Connect model, realizing that the key to achieving one's goals lies in making a connection between one's rational and emotional qualities. As I was thinking about Frank, I suddenly realized that the Courage model could help him. I immediately applied these insights to the work I did with Frank. After only a few sessions, his energy returned, and he reshaped his life, switched jobs, and became a very successful director and father.

Present

We frequently come up against boundaries in business, science, politics, companies, religions, and leadership. The boundaries we experience, however, are often within ourselves. We can only surpass these boundaries when our reason and emotions come together and form a new capacity we call seeing. This moment of seeing or insight can be full of tension. The discomfort that's created can lead us to retreat to our comfort zone and rely on either reason or emotion. If we feel more comfortable using reason, we may come up with some great ideas but be unable to act on them. On the other hand, if we rely on our emotions, we may respond impulsively and without much thought.

But overcoming the tension between reason and emotions and using these capacities simultaneously will lead to breakthrough insight. In a moment of seeing we are able to embrace these tensions and overcome them, suddenly knowing precisely what to do.

The power of seeing gives us the courage to find our way through the discomfort, tensions, and barriers from the differences in life. In this book we hope to help leaders steer through this exciting and increasingly complex world and achieve insight and action in the midst of differences, paradoxes, and complexity. It takes courage to see the world as it is. It takes courage to use the power of seeing and be a seeing-driven leader. This book shows how leaders can develop the ability to see (insight) and use the tension of differences to help others to see and overcome differences in their own business units, companies, and lives.

A Unique Model

We are the first in the world to present this unique model. An easy-in, easy-out tool, the Courage to Connect model describes how to achieve insight by connecting reason and emotion and overcoming the tension between them. It also looks at how individuals can develop their own leading and seeing abilities. This is an easy, fun way to develop leadership and transform workplaces, by seeing and overcoming the tensions and boundaries of change within companies and beyond. This book is full of real examples that show how other leaders have used the power of seeing to transform their companies.

We recently realized that it was time to develop our Courage to Connect model in greater detail and share it with the world so that more people could benefit. Together we created the book that lies in front of you. Our model is about being successful and making dreams come true. In the end, it is about love.

A Tried and Tested Approach

The Courage to Connect is an approach with tools that has been used by multinational companies in many countries, at all levels of the organization, and in many different branches and situations. The approach stimulates entrepreneurship and helps companies make major transformations and achieve clear strategy and shared action, thereby attaining great results. This book deals with applying the Courage model. It is about finding the courage to connect with ourselves, our surroundings, and the world around us. We hope to get companies to reach beyond their current goals so that they will use their leadership to positively impact world problems such as safety, the environment, poverty, and discrimination.

The Courage model tackles negative forces and uses this energy for positive growth. This book will help you to integrate this unique approach into your surroundings or your organization.

Leadership in the Twenty-first Century

Leaders in the twenty-first century need the world's support. Leadership is not a game. Leaders were once taught to keep their distance, but are now expected to be more sensitive and show more feeling. They are now trying to be more open and have contact with their people but at the same time run their business and be professional. They need help with this — after all, they have our future in their hands. We have to help business leaders first get in touch with themselves, and then with their surroundings and the outside world, so that issues like safety, quality, the environment, poverty, discrimination, and our freedom can be dealt with integrally as *the* themes of the twenty-first century.

From Self-leadership to Leading the Company

By way of our simple and practical approach, we show leaders how they can walk the path of strategic actions with a soul and entrepreneurship. Once achieved, self-leadership and entrepreneurship can lead to large transformations — to leading others (emotional issues) and leading the organization (rational issues) — transformations we've coached business leaders on for more than a decade. We also address how leaders can overcome tensions between different parts of the company and develop clear strategy with soul that others can support. Additionally, if we help leaders first get in touch with themselves and then with their environment, they will truly have the time and means to impact the world for good.

CHAPTER 1

An Introduction to Insight

New Mindset

Bill (57, CEO of a multinational food company): "My problem was that my team had lost its spirit. My colleagues were doing their jobs like routines. They had lost interest in what really mattered in our business: we had to change, grow, and innovate. I had to do something, but what and how? I just didn't know."

Although Bill is not completely satisfied with his work, he does not see exactly what is wrong, what to do, or even how to find the answers he seeks. He does not change his situation . . .

Every once in awhile you hear about people who cannot take action. They don't do what they really want to do. But aren't we all in that situation occasionally?

This book will help you turn your plans and dreams into action. It will help you bring into focus what you, deep inside, already know about yourself.

"I was afraid that if I tried some new program with my colleagues, if I challenged them, they would take it as criticism and become defensive. I also thought they would criticize whatever I did and think it was silly."

Bill knows that he should change — or at least that he should change something. He thinks about it often. He has considered a lot of options and ways he could change. But he cannot choose and he does not act.

Don't we often stay trapped in a situation or stick to certain behavior that we would like to change but never do? We are too tied up in work and daily life to be aware of what we really want.

Everyone knows someone who has broken out of a less than satisfactory situation and changed his or her way of living and working, often after a drastic experience such as a life-threatening event. When you talk to these people, they appear to have grasped exactly what their success and happiness depend on. Some people call this kind of realization a "gut feeling," "insight," or "intuition." In this book we have chosen to use the term "seeing." But whatever you call it, it is something real and very useful.

You don't have to wait for a major shake-up, however, to break free from your routine. You can use the Courage to Connect model to begin "seeing," gain insight into your dreams, and proceed to act.

Terry (46, general manager of a personal product company): "Our business was in a steady market — at least, that's how it seemed to be. We were all happily doing the same thing year after year.

"However, when we took a closer look at our figures and analyzed our market, we found out that if our top line didn't grow soon, our bottom line would collapse. In other words: we had to grow, otherwise we would have no future.

"I then realized that I needed a transformation process to change our business and to change the way we were doing business. We had to reinvent our markets. But in order to do so, and to get my people committed to do so, they needed to be both intellectually and emotionally connected to that transformation process. In other words, they all needed a new mindset. I knew it was my job to offer this to them."

Charles (38, firm director): "We have to answer questions such as: How can I retain my share? How can we stop the market from declining? How can we reduce costs without compromising quality and safety? How can we reduce costs and innovate at the same time?"

Moments of Seeing

At one time, people believed in a flat Earth and were afraid that beyond a certain point they would fall off the edge of the world. After experiencing some resistance, Copernicus' idea of a round Earth led to a complete turnaround in people's view of the world: it turned the world upside down. Discoveries such as these have changed the course of history.

By analogy, a moment of "seeing" or insight can change an individual's life forever. When you realize why you act or react the way you do, you will not only suddenly become aware of this new insight, but you will also be able to change your actions.

Seeing and intuition become most valuable when you are faced with problems and can't think of any solutions, because your normal and comfortable ways of thinking are letting you down.

Which problems are you facing now? Do you want to innovate in a saturated market? Do you have the right answers to a possible recession? Do you want your people to achieve entrepreneurship? Is your management able to get it done? Are you unhappy in your present job? Or do you want to become a top leader and a loving father or mother and partner all at the same time?

Perhaps you, like Bill in our first example, have no clue how these dreams could be turned into reality. But perhaps that is because you are thinking in terms of a flat Earth.

Business as Usual?

We believe that in this rapidly changing world, with all the information that bombards us, there is an urgent need to challenge our normal ways of doing business and handling our lives. We believe that we can't reach today's audacious business goals just by making some incremental adjustments. We won't achieve our ambitious personal targets by going about things the way we always have.

If "business as usual" is the way to go about realizing your dream, why aren't you where you want to be? The answer lies not in adjusting your dream to the situation, but in using your capabilities to achieve your dreams. We feel that there is a call for a Copernican breakthrough in thinking about both reaching our business goals and looking at our lives.

Overcoming Differences

Think about the way you tend to react when faced with different options. We often have a standard way of solving problems. Consider the way in which Bill handles tensions here:

Bill: "We had a number of fifty-year-old employees. They didn't function the way they should have. They didn't respond well to the changes in our company and also played games with our younger managers. We felt pestered by them. Behind our backs they stirred up strife among everybody. What could we do with them? Firing them was not an option; in our company that would have created a lot of tension and it goes against our values and beliefs. So what do we normally do? We send them to another training session and give them an even bigger leased car. We don't really come up with a solution — it's just a partial compromise.

"It was only after realizing that nobody was really benefiting from this solution, not the business or the employees, that I changed my attitude. I helped the older employees with their fears, although I referred to these as barriers. I did this so they couldn't skirt around the issue by saying that they didn't have any fears. The barriers I referred to, and indirectly the fears, were about losing pension rights if they were fired. An additional barrier experienced by the employees was knowing that change could be exhausting and could cause a lot of conflicts and political games. I helped them with their barriers (fears!) and the discomfort they felt about the future changes of our company.

"Only after having dealt with these barriers were we able to look at certain priorities they had to establish and work that had to be done within fixed time frames. We also set very clear consequences for when those targets weren't reached. What a difference! This was a real win-win solution."

Bill and the employees reached a solution by confronting the fears and tensions of the situation.

When confronted with a problem of conflicting needs, most people will try to reach a compromise. But in most cases better solutions — like the one created by Bill — are possible and attainable. In order to arrive at a win-win situation, we have to be aware of the needs, goals, fears, and tensions of the people involved.

Without even being aware of it, we often settle for imperfect solutions, and this becomes a barrier to problem solving. Such habits make us half as effective and thus half as successful as we could be. This not only applies to different opinions between people, but also to choices we make on a daily basis.

Differences between people, but also different options for

choices and interests in your own life, may provide the basis for creating a more positive kind of energy. Instead of using your energy to reach a compromise or play political games, it may be directed toward quicker and sharper, more powerful solutions and decisions toward goals you want to reach. But you need "round-Earth seeing" to achieve this.

Using Differences to Your Advantage

If you seize the opportunities before you, you can do things you didn't imagine could be possible. But do you dare to break your old habits? Create a passion for growth in yourself and others? Use all your capabilities as well as those of others? Use the differences in yourself and in others to create a better kind of energy?

This may sound strange, difficult, or even obvious, but you don't need a complicated theory or long checklists to achieve this. Once you gain new insight and breakthrough thinking, it will become second nature.

The Courage to Connect philosophy will help you find your own answers.

Going Beyond Strategic Action

Every individual has two basic qualities: reason and emotion. There is a natural tension between them because they are so different from one another. Perhaps you have even been trained to develop these qualities independently of each other. Perhaps you have been told that you have to open up and be more sensitive, or, instead, that your emotions are intelligent. You may have taken training courses on developing your emotional side, or you've read a book about developing your analytical skills. Such approaches can be valuable. Usually, you are stimulated to develop your less developed side and enhance one quality so that you can become a more effective person.

This book, however, is not about developing reason and emotion separately from each other. We believe that the key to your success lies in integrating and even going beyond reason with emotion. To explain how this works, we will introduce a model: the Courage to Connect. With Courage it will become clear how these two basic qualities work and what happens if you connect them and overcome the tensions between the two. After discussing the model, we will introduce a very useful tool that we call the Dream Agenda. This tool will help you train yourself in becoming more and more connected.

This connected behavior leads to success in all aspects of your life: for instance, in achieving growth in saturated markets, opening new markets, having the right answer in a declining economy, giving presentations, becoming an entrepreneur, or in building a fulfilling family life. Connected behavior handles the tension that explodes due to differences in situations, and among people, interests, and visions. It even overcomes the tension between the rational and the emotional — the hard and soft issues in life. It will provide you with a key to success and happiness. And best of all, it's fun.

General Overview

In the first diagram we present the complete Courage to Connect model and how the chapters guide you through it.

The human being is a super-integrated system and overcomes the tension and barriers

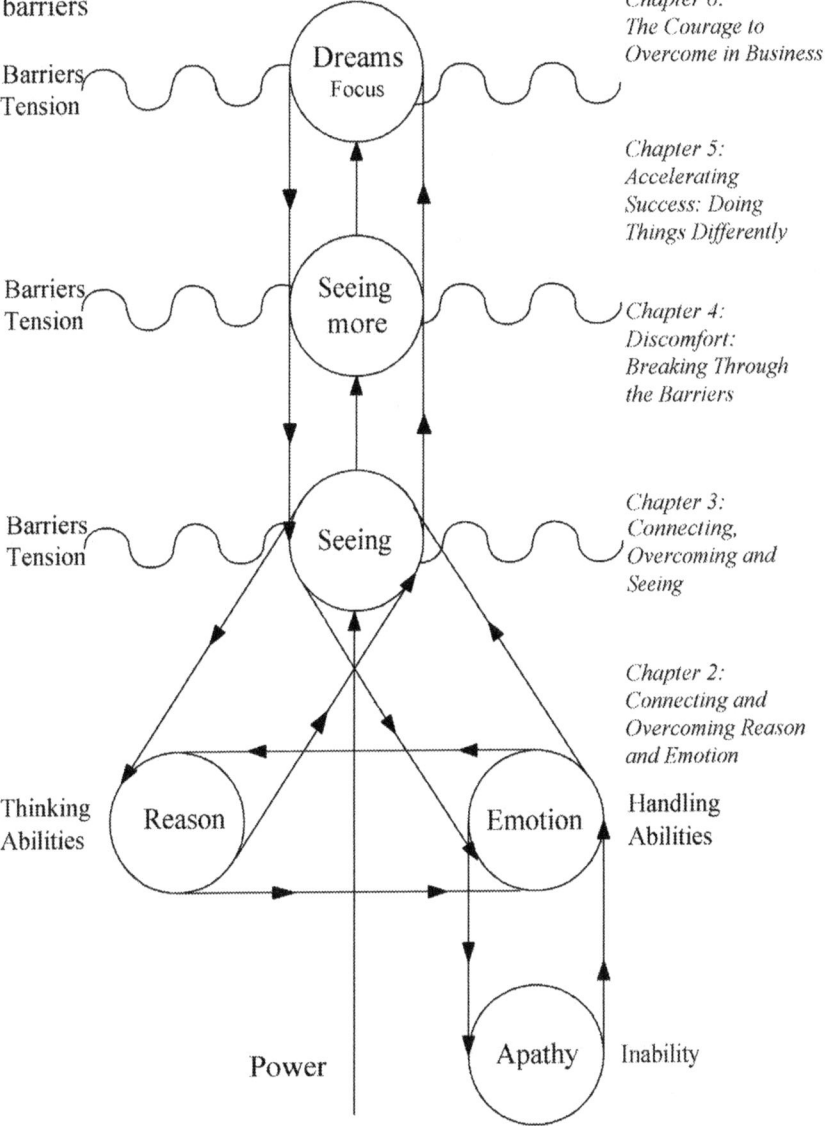

Barriers
Tension

Dreams
Focus

Seeing
more

Seeing

Barriers
Tension

Barriers
Tension

Thinking
Abilities

Reason

Emotion

Handling
Abilities

Power

Apathy

Inability

Chapter 6:
The Courage to
Overcome in Business

Chapter 5:
Accelerating
Success: Doing
Things Differently

Chapter 4:
Discomfort:
Breaking Through
the Barriers

Chapter 3:
Connecting,
Overcoming and
Seeing

Chapter 2:
Connecting and
Overcoming Reason
and Emotion

How This Book Is Set Up

Throughout this book you will become acquainted with characters who will share their vision and experience with the Courage model. You have already met Bill, Charles, and Terry; in the next chapter some others will join us. These personalities are based upon people who have worked with the Courage model for quite a while. Throughout the book they will present their experiences, troubles, and successes, but first let's cover some information about the content of each chapter.

Chapter 2:
Connecting and Overcoming Reason and Emotion

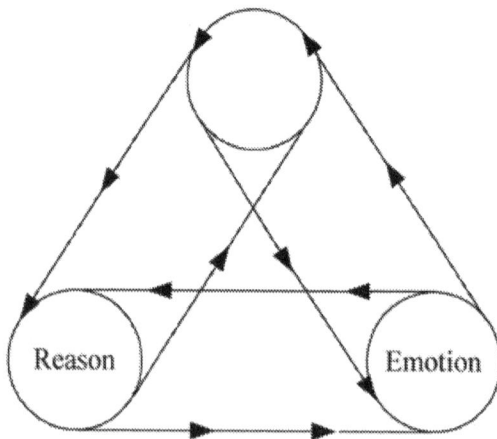

First you will get an overview of the basic abilities that are distinguished in the Courage model: reason and emotion. We will also refer to these abilities as R and E. Explore yourself and your own limits. Learn from real-life stories and become more aware of your own abilities.

Chapter 3:
Connecting, Overcoming, and Seeing

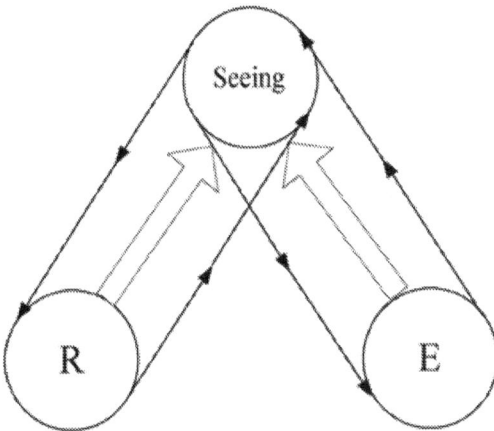

As we arrive at the heart of the Courage to Connect model, we will explain the connection between reason and emotion in more detail. At the moment we connect these two basic capacities, we experience a new ability, "seeing." How do you connect your reason with your emotion in order to experience seeing? What do you need to make the connection?

We will also talk about your dreams. What do you want to achieve? Consider all aspects of your life: what market share do you want to achieve next year(s)? What do you want to get out of your next team meeting? What do you want to achieve in your personal relationships?

Chapter 4:
Discomfort: Breaking Through the Barriers

Making the connection — the fitting together of those two basic capacities to create seeing — can present discomfort, barriers, and tension and as a result can lead one to retreat to the dominant, familiar side: reason or emotion.

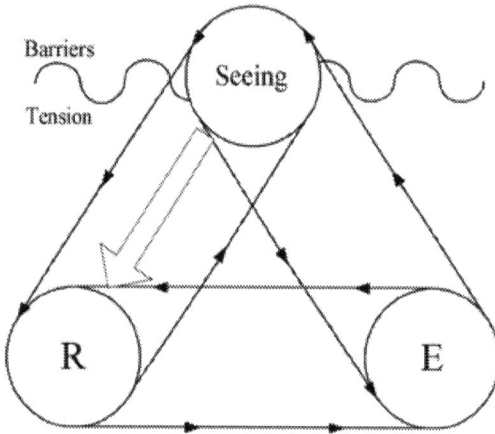

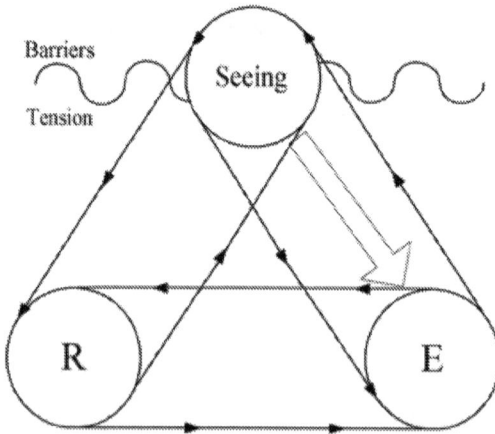

When you make your dreams explicit, you might start feeling pretty uncomfortable: "Achieving that market share is not humanly impossible!" "I can never change the strategy of the business!" "I am a total failure in bed!"

In this chapter, we will introduce a tool to tackle your tension, a tool you can use to overcome the tension of connecting your reason and your emotion (or the other way around) to create seeing.

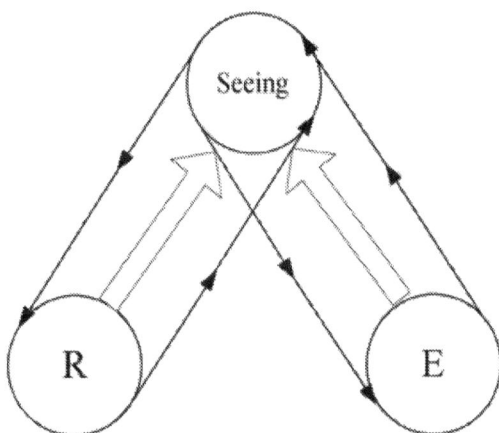

This tool to overcome tensions and barriers is tough and simple at the same time. It is tough in that you will be confronted with the tension and barriers within yourself; it is simple in that you will understand how it works within mere seconds. When you can handle the tension, barriers, and discomfort and use them successfully, then you can come to seeing more. You will no longer retreat to your reason or your emotions when you feel uncomfortable.

Chapter 5:
Accelerating Success: Doing Things Differently

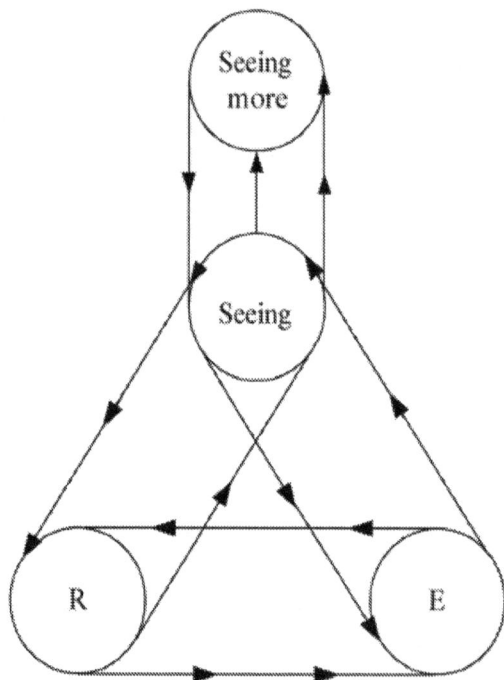

When you get to a successful R and E connection and cope well with the barriers and tensions that come with the connection, you can achieve more seeing without these tensions forcing you to retreat to your reason or your emotion. Once you start using the tool, you won't stop. You will find that the sky is the limit and that life becomes an adventure. You will start searching actively for your own barriers. In the fifth chapter, we will talk about speeding up the process toward seeing and gearing up for your success.

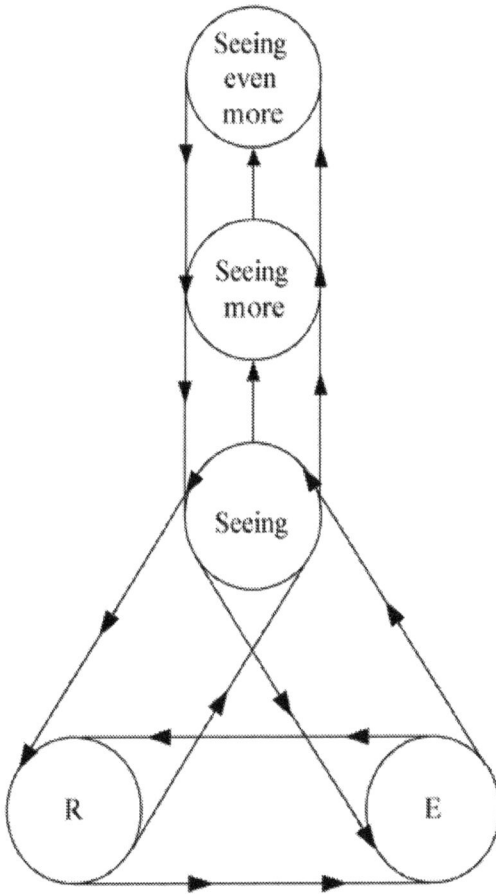

Chapter 6: The Courage to Overcome in Business

In the last chapter you will get a view of how the Courage model leads from self-leadership to leading others and from leading the organization to leading the company as a whole, integrating it all. We first see self-leadership and entrepreneurship as a successful integration and connection of R and E issues. R issues are organizational issues like planning things (tactical level), setting goals (strategic level) and reaching dreams (entrepreneurial/top level). And

E issues are getting other people to own their problems, arrive at a shared vision on the problems, and create a viable solution. We see the growth from manager (tactical) to leader (strategic) to top leader (entrepreneurial).

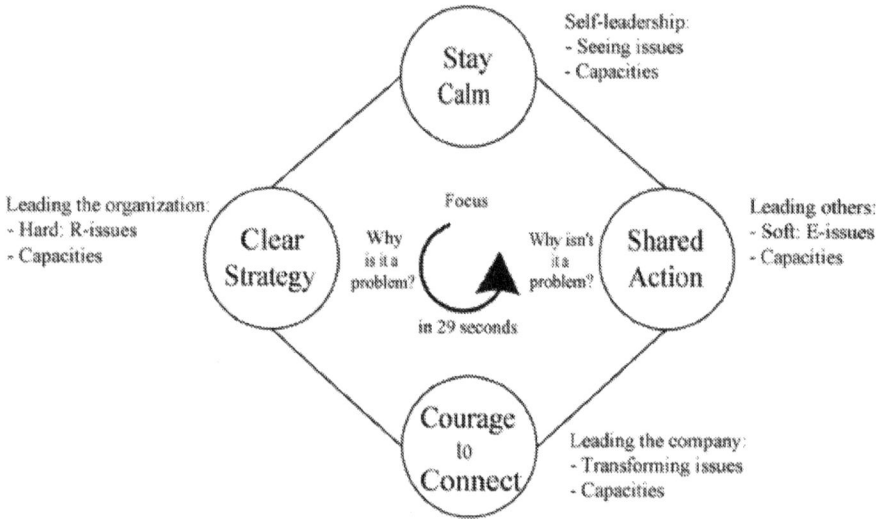

Frequently Asked Questions

Obviously, you will encounter some practical problems along the way, such as resistance or a lack of discipline on your part. How do you use the Courage to Connect approach to deal with such problems? How do you encourage others to work with this model so that you can share experiences and this new language? We will give you some practical advice on how to cope with issues like these.

Summary

We will briefly describe the whole model again, thus providing an overview of the process.

CHAPTER 2

Connecting and Overcoming Reason and Emotion

Creating Awareness

Human nature may be characterized by two major qualities: reason and emotion. Reason is the ability to think logically. It is an ability that helps us structure causes and consequences of problems and behavior. According to reason, if A occurs, then B will occur. Providing all kinds of logical rationality, reason helps us draw logical, valid conclusions. This is quite helpful and often even indispensable.

Emotion is an ability having to do with feelings. It is at the center of our actions, because it is through emotion that people do things. We move, act, and react to circumstances only when our emotions are involved. Love, desire, anger, and disappointment are some of the forces that drive action.

Although everybody is endowed with both reason and emotion, in some people the emotional side is better developed, while other people are more rational.

Robert (27) and Jane (25) are both project managers in an IT company. When Jane carries out a project, she gives it a lot of thought. She gathers a lot of data by collecting information from written sources and discussing the subject matter with other people. She comes up with many different conceptual ideas for the project.

However, she often finds it difficult to make decisions that will achieve real results and has trouble proceeding to action. She predominantly uses her rational side.

Robert's approach, on the other hand, is very action oriented. When he starts working on a project, he immediately organizes a meeting and starts putting things in motion. But he frequently does this in a disorganized manner, without any direction or thought. Often his projects are very chaotic and full of drama. He primarily uses his emotional side.

As is evident from these somewhat exaggerated examples, using one quality to the exclusion of the other prevents you from being effective.

Obviously, you will emphasize reason or emotion depending on the situation you are in. When you face an important decision involving many options, you might prefer to use your rational side, while during a brainstorm session you might put more emphasis on your emotional side.

You will get an indication of which quality you use most by filling out the evaluation below. Perhaps you will even be surprised by the outcome.

The purpose of the evaluation—and in fact this whole chapter — is not to divide individuals into two distinct categories of rationally and emotionally driven people but rather to clarify what kind of behavior or which skills stem from which quality. If you learn to recognize such behavior and skills, you can become more aware of the two basic qualities. You will be able to see under what circumstances you rely on your reason and under what circumstances you rely on your emotions. Moreover, you can learn to recognize this in other people as well.

Do You Have a Rational or an Emotional Bias?

For each question choose the answer that resembles you the most. There are no right or wrong answers. Don't think about these statements for too long.

When I'm facing a deadline:
R   I begin with structuring the process
E   I start handling the problem

When making a report:
R   I research the information in a structured way
E   I just start writing and see where it leads

When I have doubts:
R   I feel uncomfortable and imagine all the things that could go wrong
E   I feel very uncomfortable and make a decision to get rid of this feeling

When I am faced with a number of tasks, I do them:
R   One after another
E   In a random order as they come my way

When I'm under stress:
R   I consider all the possibilities and options for a long time
E   I make a quick decision without really thinking about it

Your score: number of ____R ____E

Reason

If you have more answers in the R column, your rational side might be your strongest side. Do you like to collect all the facts before making a decision? Do you plan ahead and work systematically? Do you think for a long time when you have to make difficult decisions? Do you prefer relying on your thinking and consider the options over and over again?

Emotion

If you have more answers in the E column, your emotional side might be the strongest. Do you base decisions on feelings rather than arguments? Do you sometimes act on impulse? Do you make decisions quickly? Do you sometimes lose your temper and regret it later on?

What kind of behavior belongs to your rational side? And what kind to your emotional side? By way of illustration, we will present some characteristics of people with a strong preference for one of the two basic qualities.

Rational Qualities

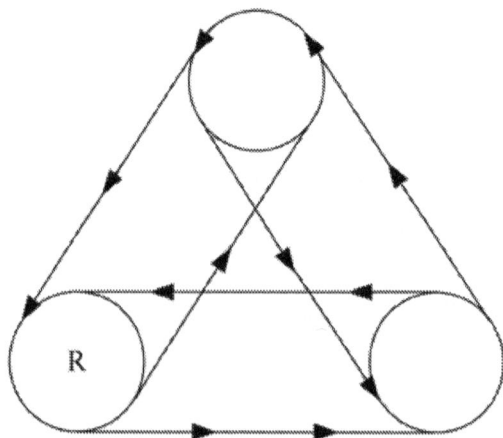

If your strength lies with your rational side, you might recognize yourself in Diana:

Diana (28, commercial manager of a real estate company): "I have good planning skills and can really think a lot about running the business. But I have difficulty meeting deadlines. I find it hard to make decisions, so I keep gathering information. I only trust figures. In meetings I use a lot of spreadsheets to convince others. Most of the time I keep going back and forth over problems in my mind. I never make a snap decision."

Can you identify with Diana and do you recognize her reasoning? These qualities often contain a downside. Diana describes her weaknesses as follows:

"I neglect my gut feeling and spend too much time on information gathering when I should be making decisions. I can also become very argumentative: I leave little room for other people's opinions because I always want to be right. I can't persuade people to do things for me. I keep a lot of distance in my relationships."

When you rely on your strong side too much, it may become your weakness. Diana's strengths at times make her inflexible and less efficient because she takes too long to come to a decision. Rationally oriented people display some of the following characteristics:

Weaknesses of rationally strong people:

- Spend too much time making (weighty) decisions
- Often fail to act
- Keep gathering information, do more research, arrange more meetings
- Have difficulty trusting their gut feelings
- Can't take rapid action on the basis of seeing
- Tend to become inflexible
- Have difficulty making up their minds
- Keep too much distance
- Remain an outsider
- Others lose their interest in them

Strengths associated with rationally strong people:

- Strong planning skills
- A tendency to structure and plan ahead
- Information-gathering abilities
- Analytical skills
- Stay calm
- Meet deadlines
- Need to weigh pros and cons all the time
- Hunger for knowledge

How to Use Your Rational Side More Effectively

If you are rationally oriented, you have a strong predisposition to using logic. You can be called R-driven. You will often try to suppress your emotions and prefer to use your rational and thinking abilities. However, suppressing your emotions does not mean you have eliminated them. On the contrary, your suppressed emotional side will keep you from functioning optimally. By using rational arguments only, without appealing to emotions, you cannot create ownership of an idea or action and passion for yourself or others. You will not succeed in leading your organization into more effective results and a better position.

A first step toward creating more effective behavior is to make better use of your emotional side and develop both qualities in tandem. You will become more effective if you try to turn toward your less developed side. This may sound like a paradox, but you can try to use them both. You will find that these two seemingly contradictory qualities reinforce one another. By involving your emotional side, you will find that different solutions arise from different angles.

If you are a rationally oriented person, the following don'ts and dos will help you begin to use your emotional side by allowing your emotion and reason to work in tandem.

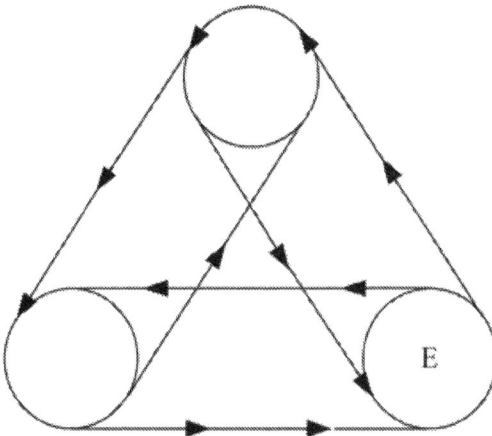

Activating Your Emotion

Don't:

- Search for more information when you know it won't make any real difference
- Try to rationalize all your decisions
- Consider emotions as soft or inferior
- Look immediately at the "what ifs"
- Endlessly weigh one option against another
- Postpone decisions

Do:

- Try to "see" exactly what is going on without rationalizing endlessly
- Try to rely more on what you see instead of the usual resources like spreadsheets, figures, and data
- Try to say what you really feel about the situation: say, "I feel bad about it, because . . ."
- Write down your top three priorities
- Write down your focus
- Be aware that every decision has advantages and disadvantages but that at one point you will have to make a decision and act (you can always correct a mistake later)
- Try to believe what you see
- Find a relaxing situation and try to think of nothing at all
- Take away your discomfort with the Dream Agenda exercises in Chapter Four

Exercises for Activating your Emotion

1. In your mind, go to a favorite place from your childhood.
   Try to see this situation as clearly as possible. Are you inside

or outside the house? Are you alone or are you with others? What is happening? In what atmosphere? What do you feel?

2. If you're in a room, look to the window; look at the shapes, then the corners. Follow the lines of the window with your eyes. Now look at a living thing: a plant, a tree, a person, or an animal. What do you see? Do you see color?

3. Please imagine you are preparing yourself for a meeting. Visualize yourself making all kinds of handouts. Put the sheets of paper in a folder and put them in your suitcase. On your way to the meeting, visualize throwing the suitcase into a river or wastebasket or visualize burning the suitcase. Then imagine you are at the meeting, standing in front of the group. How do you feel? What is your focus? Then, complete this sentence: "I have no handouts, but I can . . ."

Emotional Qualities

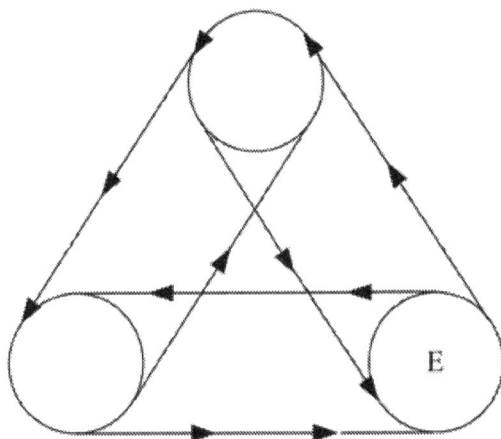

If your strength is your emotional side, you might recognize yourself in Chris:

Chris (29, marketing manager in a personal care business):
Colleagues define him as a spontaneous person with great
communication skills and empathy. He knows how to convince oth-
ers and makes his decisions quickly. When Chris feels that he is
going in the right direction he acts immediately. However, he can be
unfocused from time to time, and loses track of what he really wants
to do. At times he can hurt people with what he says. For example,
in a difficult situation he can make a phone call in anger, regretting
what he did as soon as he hangs up.

Or take a look at Edward.

Edward (24, financial consultant and student of business econom-
ics): "My work and study involve mainly rational activities. At home,
once in awhile, I can become very impulsive. I suddenly feel like I
don't want to think anymore, that I just have to work with my hands!
In a mood like that, I once trimmed a tree with little pink blossoms
that my girlfriend really loved until there weren't any branches left.
It never recovered. In the next exam period I weeded the garden. At
least, I thought it was weeded, until the next spring when I noticed
that all the plants were gone as well."

If you are like Chris and Edward and have a strongly developed
emotional side, you may possess some of the qualities listed below.

Strengths of people who rely on their emotions:
- Make rapid decisions
- Take action quickly
- Use feeling and empathy, and are thought to be approachable
  and good communicators

- Know how to reach, activate, motivate, and stimulate people
- Take problems in stride
- Strong social skills
- Spontaneous
- Good at starting things

Just like rational qualities, emotional qualities come with a downside. Chris describes his weaker points as follows:

"Sometimes my rapid actions lack a sound foundation, which is why I struggle with strategic planning. When I work on a large project, I sometimes lose track of the final goal and get confused by unforeseen situations. And when I am too busy, I can make mistakes in my hasty decisions and then get so frustrated that I lash out at people."

Chris's strength lies in acting quickly, but sometimes this hampers his planning; his actions tend to lack structure. Emotionally oriented people often show some of the following weaker points.

Weaknesses of people who rely on their emotions:
- Careless actions
- Actions tend to lack structure
- Have difficulty meeting tight schedules
- Struggle with strategic focus
- Tend to lose control
- Have difficulty focusing on their goal
- Impulsive behavior
- Regret behavior later
- Difficulty finishing things

How to Use Your Emotional Side More Effectively

If your emotional side is your strength, you can be called E-driven. Every new event triggers a new emotional reaction. This can make your behavior impulsive, chaotic, and less effective. A person driven by emotion alone might yield to uncontrolled passion and be blinded by fury. Afterwards, such people tend to regret their hasty decisions. Imagine acting on an impulse and giving your car to a beautiful woman, only to see her move on to greener pastures the next day. Or imagine firing your best sales manager after a petty argument and having to cope with a series of lost opportunities in the aftermath.

The feelings that provoke such behavior, however, are not meaningless: you shouldn't forget why you were so generous in giving away your car or so angry that you fired your best salesperson. However, if you cope with your feelings in a more connected way, you may use the energy released by such feelings as a means to move toward your goals (increase your sales), instead of pulling away from them.

A first step to more effective behavior is to make better use of your rational side and develop E and R qualities in tandem. You will become more effective if you try to use both sides by involving your rational side more.

Activating Your Reason

If your emotional side is your primary strength, how can you make better use of your rational side?

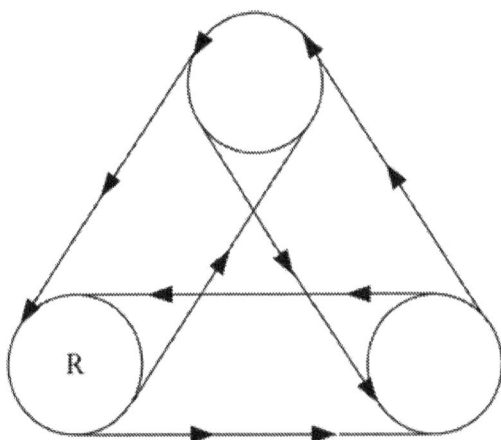

Don't:

- React impulsively when a bad or new situation arises
- Avoid information
- Repress your emotions
- Grab the phone when you are mad or send an angry e-mail immediately

Do:

- Set priorities and focus again
- Do something physical before taking action, such as washing your hands under cold water
- Write down three things you want to achieve
- Structure your daily habits
- Determine what your top three priorities are each day
- Try to recognize the situations in which you allow yourself to be led by your emotions
- Close your eyes: see a big ocean and run toward it

Exercises for Activating your Reason

1. Close your eyes. In your mind run very fast to the sea. There is a big storm. Open the doors in your head and let the storm blow

through your head for some time. Let it blow your feelings away. Close the doors again. Focus on what you want. Write it down.

2. Close your eyes. Visualize the person you have a problem with and call him or her names. Say everything you want and say why you feel the way you do.

3. Close your eyes. Imagine you are standing on the beach. Dig a very deep pit. Throw in all your negative emotions, such as anger, sadness, frustration, and betrayal. Close the pit again. Focus on what you want.

Bouncing Back and Forth Between R and E

Everyone is gifted with these two qualities and has a tendency to use one of them more readily. But in the end you always need the weaker or less familiar side if you are to create more seeing and focus. Combining R and E has something to do with timing and balance between the two. Being too quick can mean that you are too emotional, but being too slow can mean that you are too rational.

There is also a natural tendency to bounce back and forth between reason and emotion without developing "seeing" or focus. Consider the following thought process:

Example: Stuck Bouncing Between R and E

You walk into your room and suddenly realize it is a mess. You had not seen the mess for months, so suddenly you're experiencing an integrating moment of your reason and your emotion. But once you make the realization you retreat to your R and then swerve to your E and then go back to your R again and so on. It goes something like this:

Rational: "I must make a plan for how to clean up this mess. But I don't have the time for it."

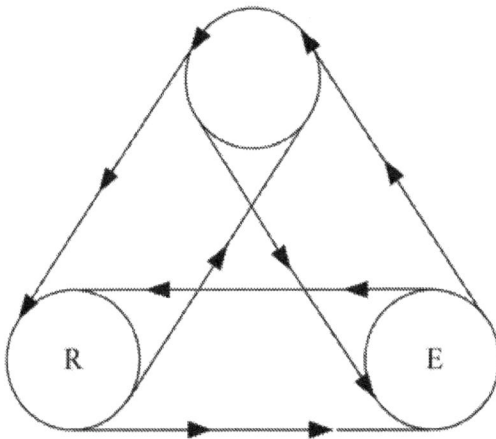

Emotional: "I feel bad about how this looks, so I'll start cleaning up immediately."

When you begin to clean, you create an even bigger mess. You return to reason to create some order.

Rational: "Where do I begin? When I start planning, I don't have time to clean and when I start cleaning I don't see any progress because I don't have a plan!"

Emotional: "This is terrible!"

Overcoming Apathy and the Negative Energy Resulting from Connecting Reason and Emotion

When you get stuck in a problem, you might go back and forth between your reason and your emotion until frustration and apathy arise. Apathy is the state in which you don't think or feel anymore. At first, you worry endlessly. You may even lose some sleep over it. Next you become emotional: angry, frustrated, and desperate. Then apathy sets in: you no longer care.

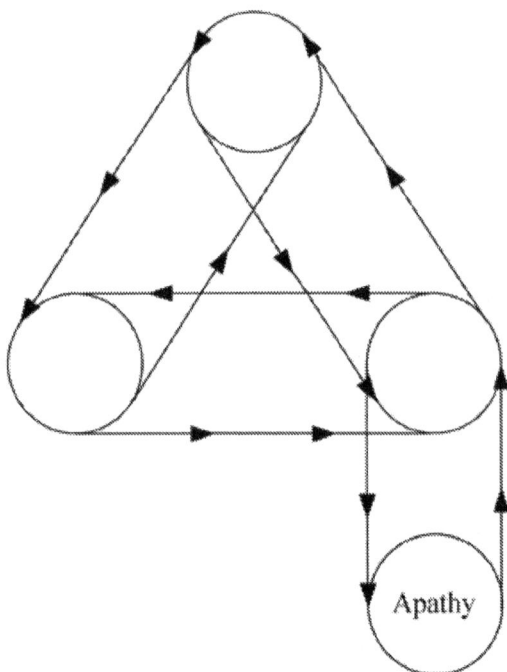

Karen (34, head of product development for a beer company): "I kept going back and forth over our new strategy because somehow it didn't feel right. After discussions with my colleagues and analysis of our market, I saw some ways in which we could improve our strategy. I began to have these conversations with our CEO in my head, because I don't dare to say 'hello' to him, let alone advise him about our strategy. I told myself that it would not interest the CEO and that other colleagues had tried to talk to him as well and didn't get an appointment, either. That way I began to lose interest in my ideas, dropped the subject, and gradually lost interest in my job as well."

Chris: "After our business moved to another town and we reorganized, a couple of energetic and needed employees left. After the move I worked very hard to get the new team on track. But I got the

---

impression that nobody was listening to me. When I shared my feel-
ings, it was taken as a sign of weakness. One day I would come home
thinking about what to do and another day I would be very emotional
about the situation. This went on for months and then I ran out of
energy. I didn't want to think about it anymore. I didn't care anymore.
I was indifferent. Even though a colleague said it would turn out well,
I felt so bad about it that I became apathetic again."

In the Courage model, apathy is linked to emotion: it is only through emotion that you can escape from apathy. If an individual is indifferent about something, rational arguments carry no force. For example, telling such a person to talk to his team members and get clarification will not produce any effect.

The Courage to Connect method is based on building up the ability to feel again. Moving out of apathy means connecting with your emotions. People who feel indifferent should try to do something that stirs up emotions. They should look at their anger, feel it again, and find a way to express it. They should try going out for dinner with a friend and talking about a new focus, taking up a new challenge, going to the movies, or doing an enjoyable or stim-ulating activity. It does not matter whether their spirits are lifted or are provoked: the important thing is that they get back in touch with their emotions.

From this point on, people who have become indifferent may be guided back to their seeing by experiencing some emotion and some reason and integrating them. Then they can take a new look at the situation, see the solution, get their focus back, and try to live again by connecting and formulating their dreams, which we will discuss later. In the case of Frank, described in the preface, this is exactly the way in which he was pulled out of his apathy.

After this digression about the part of the Courage model that deals with apathy, we return to situations in which most people usually find themselves. A crucial aspect of understanding yourself and making progress by using the Courage model involves being aware of your reason and emotion.

Successfully Overcoming Reason and Emotion: Finding the Perfect Balance

Understanding the characteristics of rational and emotional behavior can make you more aware of your own behavior and skills and those of others. Isn't the reaction of your colleague Chris somewhat emotional? How could his reaction be more effective? Isn't Diana a bit too rational in her behavior? Wouldn't she become more effective if she could make better use of her emotional side?

The next step, however, is not only to make better use of your neglected side but to make a real click between the two basic qualities. This leads to more effective behavior. In the click you will become more focused and better able to get in touch with your seeing capacities. A perfect balance may be achieved between feelings and thoughts, body language and words, chaos and order, practice and theories. The click is about successfully integrating feelings and thoughts so that you can overcome the natural barriers and tension that exist between R and E.

Exercise: Are Your Reason and Emotions in Balance?
This exercise will help you make the balance between R and E even clearer.

1. Imagine a situation at work in which you felt totally uncomfortable.
2. Describe the uncomfortable situation in some detail: What was it about? Which people were present?
3. How did you deal with the situation?
4. Make two columns, one with "reason" written at the top and one with "emotion" written at the top.
5. Look closely at what your answers to question # 3. List your behaviors under one of the two headings. For example, "I immediately said what I thought and was gesticulating wildly" and "I was too quick with the action I regretted later on" belong under the emotion heading. "I did a lot of information gathering and thinking without reaching a conclusion" and or "I was too slow with my reactions" belong under the reason heading.
6. Take a look at the two columns: they describe your behavior in that particular situation. Were your actions at that moment more rational or more emotional?

In addition to exploring your own behavior, this exercise can enable you to look at the behavior of others and understand how they use the two basic qualities.

In the next chapter, we will start connecting the two qualities and find out what happens when the connection is made.

CHAPTER 3

Connecting, Overcoming, and Seeing

What About the Facts?

Hans (51, general manager of an oil company): "When I get involved in a new business, I always notice the compelling need for change. I intuitively see where change has to take place. I just smell it. I walk around the office, talk to the staff, and then just know where things go wrong. Of course my task is to make the need for change felt in the organization. I have to help the people involved realize that they have to start their analysis."

Bill: "Peter, my successor, came to a meeting and told us: 'We should stop investing in the brand.' He withdrew all advertisements. Everyone knew that this brand had no future, but nobody dared to make the decision to stop investing in it. My team members turned red and became furious with him! They wanted facts, but Peter followed his gut instinct, and it turned out that he was right. Can you make good decisions based on just your gut feelings?"

Should your seeing be mistrusted? Is your insight as vague and elusive as many people think?

The Power of Seeing

In the Courage model, "seeing," or insight, is defined as the understanding that takes place when reason and emotion connect. Therefore, in our model, seeing is not to be defined as something soft or intangible. It is just as hard as it is soft, just as rational as it is emotional; it is the integration of both. Seeing can help you make better decisions faster and help you with the direction and implementation of what you want. Seeing without letting the tension of it throw you back to your R (which results in slow action or inaction) or E (which results in hasty action) can give you the sense of timing and action in the right direction. So, then you can have the skill to clearly define the right direction and then transform this direction into well-timed and focused action. In this way you can enlarge your focus, seeing, and strategic capacities, which you can transform into well-directed, tactical actions. Plus, it is a skill that can be practiced and improved.

In this chapter we will explain how seeing emerges and how you can recognize and develop it, achieving deeper insights and even foresight.

Power of Foreseeing

As you learn to overcome your reason and emotion and exercise the resulting ability to "see" and gain insight into difficult situations, you will begin to see more and more. The more you use the power of seeing, the better you can see what it is that you really want and gain deep insight. With this deep insight comes the ability to see further into the future and know what to anticipate and how to react. This advanced level of insight we call the power of foreseeing, or foresight.

From Insight to Foresight

Let's review this process of seeing and coming to deeper insight. The first step of seeing involves connecting your reason and emotion in order to see, and using the discomfort or tension from that situation to make insight-driven decisions. When you continue to anchor your seeing and trust your gut feeling, or intuition, you advance to the second step of seeing — insight. This second level of seeing is much less fragile and fleeting than the first step and increasingly influences your decisions. When you use this insight as a new seeing step (or a springboard for further and deeper insight) you come to a third step of seeing — foresight. In all the previous steps, you use the tension of more and more seeing to achieve foresight. So you move from the level of intuition (first seeing stage) to anchored insight (second seeing stage) to foresight (third seeing stage). At this third and most advanced level of seeing, you act in a more preventive way.

From Foresight to Prevention

From this third step of foresight you use your intuition and seeing ability to take glimpses into the future and look at long-term goals. This third stage gives you the opportunity to overcome your emotional and impulsive actions (which are E-driven), as well as procrastination or delays (which are R-driven), so that you can make decisions driven by the power of intuition, insight, and foresight. This insight-driven capacity prevents you from making too many mistakes and losing the power to act decisively or make good decisions.

The Power and Courage of Seeing the Whole

The power of seeing gives you the capacity to see things and even the world around you as an inter-related whole. It helps you learn how to use the tension of conflict to bring together reason and emotion, the hard and the soft sides of situations and issues, and see differences connected in the world. The need to overcome differences and tension extends to every person, every team, every company, every business, and the world. In each setting we need to learn to go beyond our differences, using the power of seeing to find win-win solutions. It takes courage to see how differences are connected. It takes the courage to connect to see what brings people together, rather than what divides them.

Seeing the Solution

Seeing (which you can develop to the point of foresight) is the combination of your feelings and logic when you're involved in instinctively grasping the solution to a problem. People often wonder why they did not think of such a solution before, because seeing makes it seem so obvious. Sometimes seeing is like snapping your fingers — in an instant you see what you should do or know precisely how you should solve a particular problem. But it does not necessarily involve a single moment in time: once you know how to use seeing, it can be a continuous source of behaving. Ultimately, you can become seeing-driven.

As was shown in the previous chapter, our two basic qualities of R and E make us behave differently and often drive us in different directions. Just think of when you were installing your first computer. If you started by reading the manual all the way through, it probably took some time before you got your computer working. If,

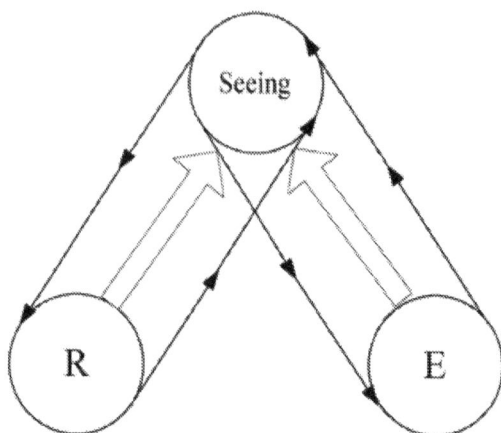

on the other hand, you just started randomly pushing keys, most likely some "fatal errors" occurred. These strategies are situated at the extreme ends of the spectrum of reason and emotion. The strategy you use depends on the situation and on your ability to use your reason and emotion at the same time.

As we have shown before, neither of the two reactions yields optimal results.

There is, however, a third way that involves learning step by step to rely on seeing. In the Courage model, this seeing is described as thinking and feeling at the same time. In Courage terms, we say that when you see you have integrated your reason and your emotion successfully.

The same thing happens when you suddenly solve a complex problem: the solution seems to present itself to you, but it is, in fact, your seeing that led the way.

Carl (29, marketing manager of a food company): "As soon as we saw our new CEO, we knew that our business would change, every element of it: competition, industry, market attractiveness, brands, and how we operated together with the trade. And the strange thing was that as soon as we got into this process, our solutions sometimes came to us intuitively: a brand manager would just walk in with the brightest plans. We all became very smart, inspired, and focused during that first period."

Jane: "I remember one time I solved a problem using the seeing. I was working on a very complex problem. We were taking a break in a meeting and I was watching the traffic near our office. Then, suddenly, the solution came to me. It just sprang into my mind. I knew what we had to do. And it turned out to be the perfect solution! It's like being a visionary."

Seeing Toward Leadership

When you ask people to tell you what they mean by seeing, you might get answers such as: "It happens in a flow of ideas," "It happens when you have a peak experience," "It's a sudden insight," "It's your sixth sense," or "It is your gut feeling." It is like being able to predict the future.

Exercise: Your Experiences with Seeing

When and in what situations have you experienced seeing? The following questions will help you explore this area:

- When was the last time you had a moment when you snapped your fingers and said, "I see it," "I got it!" or "I know it"?
- Do you listen carefully to yourself when you use phrases such as "I know what I have to do" or "I feel this is right"?
- Do you know someone who follows what he or she sees?
- Do you know people who can easily see solutions?

What Does Seeing Do for You?

Your seeing can help provide an overview of what is happening. It can help you realize what you have to do to achieve your goals and give you self-confidence.

Frank (31, buying director of a retail company): "The market one particular vendor was into experienced heavy losses with declining volumes. This company, however, became very innovative and every year the turnover increased by ten percent. It's a success story, and when I asked how they did it, it turned out that many of their solutions came from intuition. It was like magic for us."

Diana: "As soon as I started using my seeing more, I had a better overview of what I was doing, where I wanted to go, and how I could get there. I started making decisions faster and based more on what I really saw. I felt like the captain of a ship: I knew where my ship was going and how to get people on board. For the first time I felt really in charge of myself and my surroundings."

Seeing can help you understand the range of possibilities before you. You may become more inventive, innovative, or concentrated. Seeing can guide you in your focused search for information. Seeing can help you decide on the right course of action. Seeing is the essence of leadership.

Chris: "I didn't know what to do: should I find a new business partner or shouldn't I? I worried and worried, until I started trusting my seeing. I wrote down what I really wanted to achieve, not only in my business but also in my personal life. And I looked at the tension I had with what I wanted. I looked at the discomfort I was feeling while looking into the future. These goals gave me so much clarity that I started to grasp much better than before what I had to do. I just knew what was right."

Doris (54, financial director): "When I started to trust my seeing, I realized that it changed the authority I felt I carried. I didn't need to refer everything back to the board anymore; I felt more in charge of myself and my surroundings. I even began to display leadership qualities with my boss."

Seeing is your compass. If you are not in the habit of using it, it might be a bit difficult to find your true direction. But trust yourself. You always have your inner compass to guide you.

How to Connect?

Obviously, it is very convenient if your seeing just pops up now and then without your knowing where it comes from. You could be taking a bath or standing in an elevator not thinking about the problem, but like magic the solution presents itself.

But wouldn't it be even more convenient if you were capable of making the connection between your reason and your emotions yourself? If you were able to have these moments of seeing and vision whenever you needed them?

The Courage model can help you experience such moments of clarity in a more structured way. It can assist you in developing your seeing capacity. You can train yourself to become sharper and more focused.

Training Yourself

We have suggested that the tension and barriers of integrating reason and emotion can be overcome if you succeed in connecting the two. According to the Courage model, once you connect, you begin to see what you have to do and you start developing your seeing ability more.

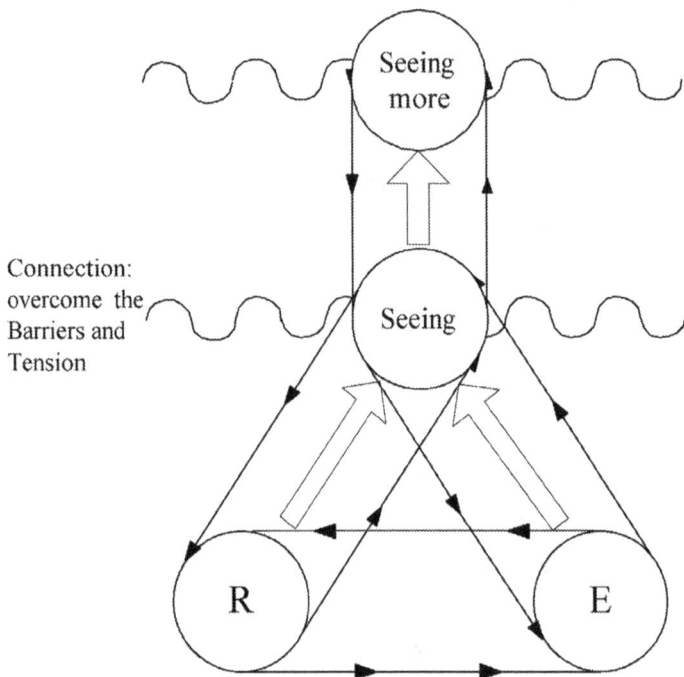

By following the two steps below you will train yourself to make the connection between R and E more easily.

Step One: Creating Awareness

The first step is to be aware of the tension that comes from seeing. How do you act when you see? Do you retreat to your emotions or to your reason? To answer these questions, you can use the tools provided in Chapter Two. Listen both to what your reason has to say and to what you feel. Do the two qualities come into conflict? If so, figure out what you really want by focusing on and formulating your dream.

Imagine: You no longer feel stimulated by your current job. If you want to obtain insight, try to become aware of the tension between your two reactions to the problem you are grappling with. Your reason comes up with arguments such as "It's okay to have a job that does not stimulate me anymore, because now I have plenty of time to spend with my family." It is your emotions that tell you, "I am not happy."

What should you do?

Step Two: Formulating Your Dream

The second step is to ask yourself what you want to achieve. By answering this question — for instance, with respect to your job — you might see more clearly than before where you want to go. Your dream might be that you want to have a stimulating job, work outside, have more spare time, enjoy yourself, be a more spontaneous and friendly person, or make more money.

Exercise: How To Focus On and Clarify Your Dream

It is your dream that makes you connect your reason with your emotion. By making your dream explicit, you channel the energy evolving from the tension of the integration into a positive direction. Subsequently, you start seeing more and more. Answer the following questions:

- What do you want?
- Is this really what you want? Bring it into clearer focus. Then bring it into even sharper focus. Is it really what you want, deep inside?

- Focus again for the final time. Write down as clearly as possible what you really want.

Focus, Seeing, and Dreams

Seeing starts developing once you become more aware of the tension of your seeing in a problem or a solution. It develops further when you formulate what you want to achieve. If you see where you want to go, you will connect your reason with your emotion and from this, more seeing follows. The energy evolving from the tension between your R abilities and your E abilities steers you in the right direction. Your thinking abilities and your handling (emotional) capacities, so to speak, integrate toward your seeing capacity. It brings the complexity into focus.

The previous chapter helped you become more aware of your reason and your emotion. Now you must become more aware of your dreams, your focus, and what you want to achieve.

Your dreams can be about anything — about business issues like double-digit growth, enjoying working with your boss (even though she is impossible), doubling your market share next year, or being the best sales manager in your company. Obviously, dreams can also be about personal goals such as establishing an even closer relationship with your partner, writing a novel (a bestseller, of course), or having a gorgeous body. Dreams can be about important life issues, but also about small, daily matters such as exercising regularly or spending less time worrying.

Without powerful dreams, your daily life might not satisfy you, and make you feel empty.

The human being is a super-integrated system
and overcomes the tension and barriers

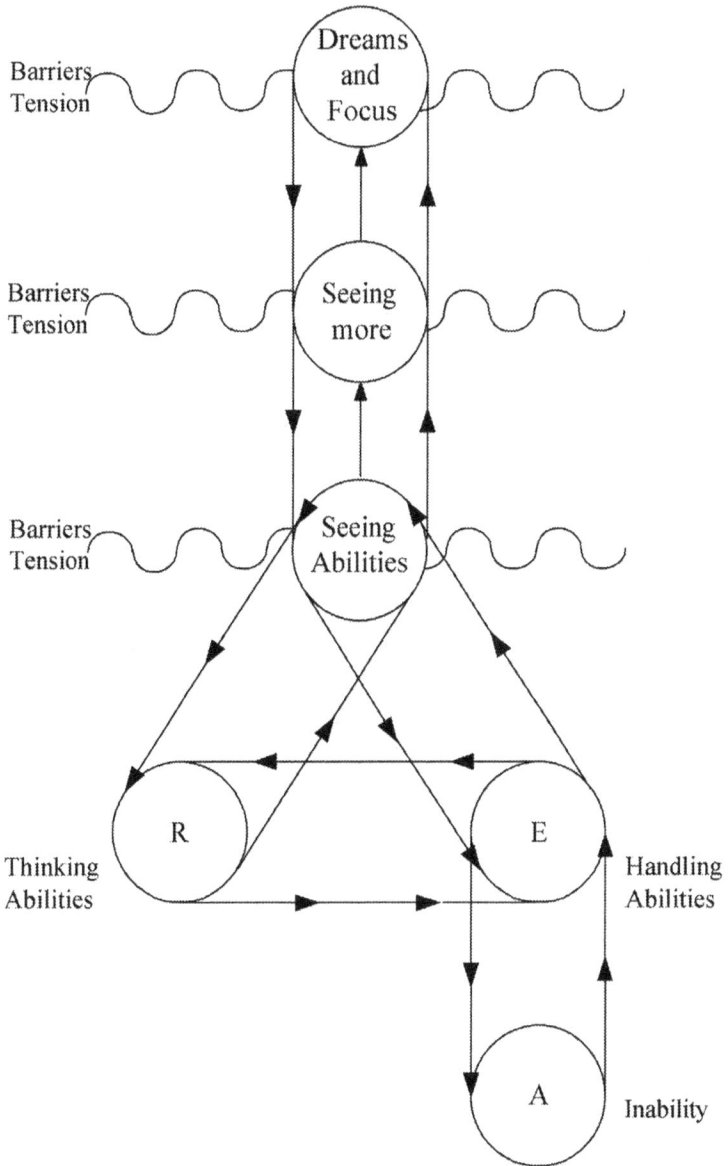

Barriers
Tension

Dreams
and
Focus

Barriers
Tension

Seeing
more

Barriers
Tension

Seeing
Abilities

R

E

Thinking
Abilities

Handling
Abilities

A

Inability

Angela (project manager in a big interior design warehouse): "I felt I wasn't focusing my energy. I didn't have a goal. Why was I working so hard? Where was it leading? What did I want to achieve?"

Robert: "I think it was just a few years ago. I had just been promoted to project manager and my life and work were going really smoothly. I was busy, running from one appointment to the other, and my forecasts and revenue models were as correct as possible. Even the people around me created an exciting environment. I earned a lot of money. But it didn't feel good. I didn't have time to live. I had financial problems and had to work late to pay all the bills. I suddenly felt I was in a kind of prison. I felt unfocused. Was this all there was in life?"

Exercise: Exploring Your Power of Seeing

These questions might not always be easy to answer. Once you find the answers, however, they may lead you to where your seeing is waiting for you. Your answers will provide a starting point; from this point on, your seeing will start telling you what to do.

- Which achievements make you feel proud of yourself?
- What would you most like to do before you die?
- What situations most frighten to you?
- What makes you feel energetic?
- At what point in time did you feel the most energetic?

Norman (44, plant manager of bakery products): "I had a personal crisis a few years ago: my marriage was not working, and at work I felt I wasn't getting the promotions I deserved. I was down and out. But now, looking back, I feel very fortunate to have gone through it. It led me to dream about what really mattered to me and what I wanted to achieve. Through that I grew as a person. I wasn't afraid to speak up, to give my opinion without necessarily having to hurt others. I feel much better now. I can cope with the stress much better and am not as nervous as I used to be. I make decisions in a more focused way, both at home (my marriage has improved a lot) but also in my job."

Chris: "There was a moment in my career when I started wondering what I was doing with my life. I was a sales manager at the time and ran from one sales event to another. I became more and more frustrated with my way of working. I felt tired all the time. I forced myself to take a step back and look at what I was doing. I concentrated on the problem and I asked myself what I wanted, what I stood for in life. I realized then that I wanted to create something of my own. It took awhile, but in the end I quit the sales job and started my own company. I feel wonderful now and I am proud of what I do."

Helping Others

After answering these questions, you may want to share your answers with others. You might also want to ask other people to work through the list. This interaction may yield some surprising answers and spur new ideas. By sharing your dreams with other people and listening to their dreams, you will start building a network of people around you who share a mutual language and a mutual way of seeing. They can offer their support when you are feeling down or when you keep bouncing back and forth between the same issues. You can help them out, too.

Dream Big, Start Small

Your dream may be described as something important, something that unfolds in front of you. To reach your dream you often have to start with small steps, which may be described as goals and things that have to be planned step by step. A dream provides focus to your goals. It allows you to align all your daily activities with a specific purpose.

Yuri (30, systems manager of an international real estate agency): "Our business was very traditional and hierarchical. When the new CEO came, he said that he wanted to change the business and turn it into a modern, inspiring company, a company that could survive future developments. He wanted to involve everybody in this. Then he initiated a whole lot of projects, company-wide events, team-building exercises, and learning conferences. Only after some time did we see that these were all steps toward his dream."

Harriet (43, team trainer of a production plant): "I now see that the changes in our factory were set out in three clear phases. First there was the breaking down of the organization and the former para-digms as a platform of change. Then the strategic program was designed. Finally it was about the implementation — reconnecting with ourselves and setting our values. I think these were three clear steps toward the realization of a dream."

More Examples of Developing Your Seeing

Developing seeing is not always that easy. The following suggestions may help you.

Don't:

- Keep gathering information again and again
- Act too quickly and without understanding the place of the solution in the total strategy
- Feel bad about it and drop your plans

Do:

- Imagine drawing a dot on the wall and throwing the point of your pencil in it
- Look outside your window and focus on something far away
- Write down what you are experiencing
- Ask yourself why what you see is okay
- Make what you see clearer
- Write down what you really see
- Write down your top priority
- Write down what makes you feel uncomfortable
- Trust yourself
- Release physical tension
- Relax your mind once in awhile
- Keep a notebook for your ideas and your experiences
- Open up to new experiences
- Be aware of the way you think, act, and feel

Seeing and Leadership

In today's business environment, there is an urgent need for leaders who radiate passion and power concerning their dreams for their companies. Leaders who are focused and know how to innovate and fight for their market share are in short supply. There is an urgent need for leaders who are committed to their dreams and subsequently use their seeing ability to direct their behavior — for leaders who connect their emotion with their reason by using and overcoming the tension that goes along with seeing and to help others to do so too.

Such leaders are intellectually convincing and emotionally appealing. By integrating both qualities, they become visionaries. They are capable of transforming their companies into flexible, dynamic, fast-growing businesses while being happy and successful people themselves.

Don't:

- Try to be too rational
- Act in an impulsive manner
- Lie to yourself
- Try to control everything
- Underestimate the power of your emotion and reason
- Stop having dreams about what you want to achieve

Jane: "We were having a difficult time with our business. Each year, it was getting harder to make a profit. We were working very hard without deriving any satisfaction from it. Two years ago, all this changed. We spent some time with our team focusing very seriously on what we wanted to achieve. We dealt with the tension that goes along with this kind of process, and slowly a picture began to emerge. With renewed energy, we started to work toward this new vision. We were driven by what we knew was the right thing to do. And we also saw very clearly how to achieve this."

Jim (29, development manager of a food company): "At the beginning of the change process in our company there was disbelief and a lot of discomfort and tension. Nobody believed the process would do any good. But in the following years, we took the steps that were laid out for us: the coaching, the workshops, the new values and beliefs, the role modeling of our CEO. We began to understand why he'd given us the chance to change. After a few years, all of us had changed. We let go of our disbelief and began to see that yes, we could make a difference."

Frustration and Apathy

It may seem surprising that not everyone is inspired and motivated to make dreams come true professionally and personally. Instead of becoming aware of the tension of integrating reason and emotion and channeling the resulting energy toward their dreams, many people allow the tension to pull them down. Instead of breaking down their barriers, they resort to old habits. Changing their behavior would result in more tension and more discomfort than they're willing to deal with. Many people remain stuck in an unsatisfactory situation out of fear of such discomfort. Some people simply give up every hope of breaking out of this vicious cycle.

Breaking through takes courage. In the next chapter we will show you how to build up such courage.

CHAPTER 4

Discomfort: Breaking Through the Barriers

I Can't Do It!

Once you have a clear concept of what you want and what your dream is, then you will you know what you need to implement and what you can achieve. You will have reached a crucial point at which your seeing can push you in the right direction to achieve tangible goals.

In the previous chapter, we explained how to go beyond the rational and the emotional to become connected. We also talked about seeing and how it may be used to define your dream and make it a reality. But the seeing that leads you toward your dream is quite fragile. It is easily disturbed by your discomfort in seeing or in the unknown and unfamiliar. You see where you want to go and the steps in front of you leading toward your goal, and then it strikes — the fear that you can't do it, you don't dare do it. Even the tension and excitement of the seeing itself can throw you back because you now know the wonderful idea that you may never implement. "My dream is wonderful," you tell yourself, "but I can't possibly achieve it. It is impossible to fulfill all the requirements that are necessary to make my dream come true."

Rose (36, HR manager of a retail organization): "When I first started this job, I wanted to help my general manager achieve his ambitious goal of setting up a whole new formula of retail shops.

However, when we started to work on the plans for implementation, I started to doubt whether I could do it. Was I capable of managing so many projects for such a large number of people? What strategy could I use to help me choose from among all the possibilities?"

Chris: "I dreamed about starting my own company, but when I realized what would be involved, I became insecure. Could I manage on my own? Could I get the right people to work with me? Could I cope with financial insecurity? To be honest, many times I just didn't think I could."

Restless Comfort

In your comfort zone, you know how to handle a situation. You simply do things the way you always have. You act according to habit. And out there at the edge of your comfort zone lies a sea of discomfort filled with unpleasant tension about all the things you have never done before and the many skills you think you are lacking.

By formulating your dreams and goals you realize that the only way to reach them is to get out of your comfort zone and overcome the barriers and tension. You know you cannot continue doing the things the way you have always done them — this will not bring you any closer to your dream. However, the mere thought of the steps you have to take makes you uneasy.

Having to act makes you feel uncomfortable. But if you are honest with yourself, you may find that you are also starting to feel a bit restless and dissatisfied in your safe comfort zone because your dream remains unfulfilled. In view of what you want to achieve, you realize that you have no choice but to dive into that sea of discomfort — embrace it, in fact.

Anthony (27, organizational consultant): "After some years work-
ing in a big company, I dreamed about starting up something on my
own. But how was I to achieve this? I thought I would never make
it. I was afraid I wouldn't be able to get enough clients. I was also
worried that if I had clients I wouldn't be able to deal with their
demands. I considered how to juggle acquisition and product
development at the same time. I feared I would get exhausted from
product development, losing energy from lack of sleep; whereas for
acquisition I was concerned that I would have to be on the ball and
be as sharp as if I had just returned from a vacation in Miami. I
worried and worried — and here I am still working for the same
boss."

The Great Discomfort

Consider the following example: Your organization is steering
through rapidly changing times. Because of business trends —
including those in globalization, IT, individualization, a possible

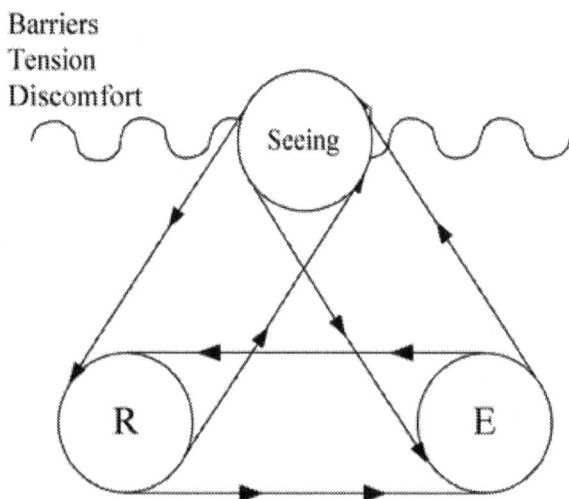

economic decline, and the facts that your products need to be replaced and that your plans and reality don't match anymore — the tensions and insecurities in your company are increasing. Your business is not showing sufficient growth. Moreover, years ago your company experienced a major disaster — the explosion of one of your business units, killing fourteen people. Fears increase by the day, yet you dream about transforming your management team into a tightly knit, efficiently working group of people who inspire your employees and enjoy working together in a safe and high-quality company that cares about environmental issues.

To achieve your dream, you will have to address some difficult issues. For example, you may see that the behavior of one of your colleagues is not constructive and he tries to force changes by playing on people's fears without integrating these with reason. He doesn't focus on the company. More importantly, you realize (albeit reluctantly) that you are not always behaving effectively yourself and you're having difficulty handling the tension.

After forming your dream, and overcoming the tension that goes along with it, you start to create goals. Mistakes you've made in the past start to take shape in your mind, and your seeing helps you realize what has been going on in your team and why you have not yet reached your goals.

The idea that you have to address these difficult issues, however, makes you feel uncomfortable because you will have to leave your comfort zone. Your discomfort expresses itself in doubt: How am I going to do this? What if they speak up and criticize the way I've been doing things? Can I handle criticism? What if I don't know what to say? What if everything turns out wrong?

Does this feel good? No!

In short, you only think about taking action. And then you feel uneasy and return to unproductive thoughts.

Discomfort Can Push You Back Into Old Behavior Patterns

Discomfort is something we want to get rid of. Our primal reaction to discomfort is to try to get away from it, return to our comfort zone, and feel safe again.

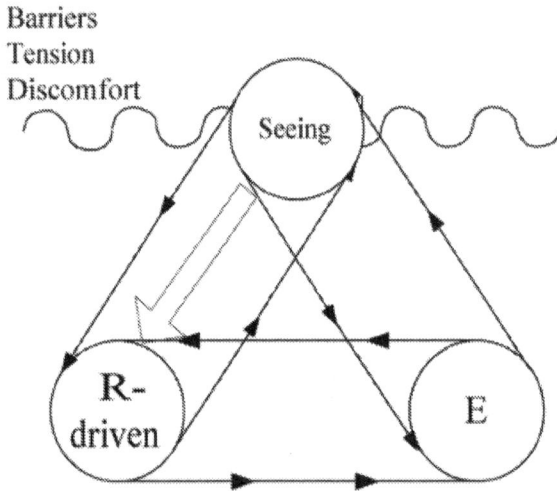

A common way to escape from discomfort is to return to your strongest side (E or R) first. A rationally driven person might make a list of pros and cons, start reasoning, and even start to prepare a presentation with lots of slides and figures with the hope of convincing others.

An emotionally driven person will tend to do something — anything — immediately and without much thought, apologizing later for what he or she has said impulsively.

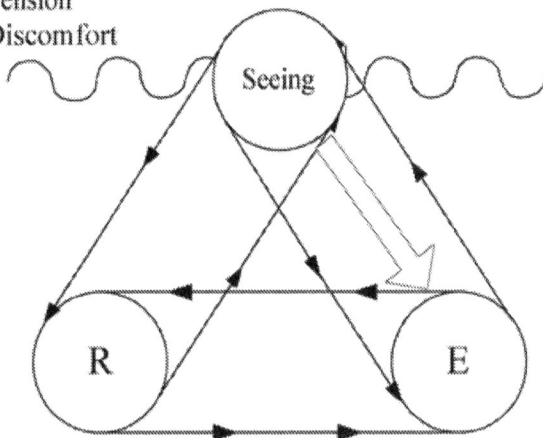

Barriers
Tension
Discomfort

Instead of relying on just one quality, you can also bounce back and forth between your R and E and get imbalanced. Oftentimes you can run out of energy and then become apathetic.

In this example, a rationally oriented person might start doubting whether it is a good idea to address individual behavior in the team: "Perhaps people won't know what to say, but then again, why shouldn't they?" Your discomfort might not vanish, but at least you are in safe territory: you feel comfortable with familiar reasoning patterns.

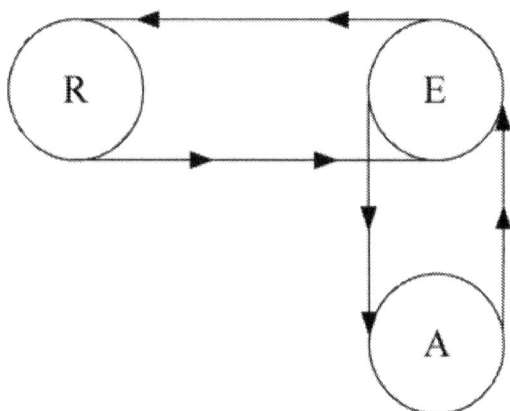

If, on the other hand, you have a strong emotional side, your discomfort might be expressed in thoughtless, impulsive behavior because you want to act on the spot to get rid of uncomfortable feelings. In this example, you might start addressing an employee's behavior without warning or in the wrong setting. Or you might ask your team member out of the blue, "So what do you think of me?" This could end up angering him and totally confusing you.

In both cases, you will not achieve your dream or act appropriately.

Diana: "What I wanted to achieve was clear: to change the strategy of our firm by focusing on a different market. But how? We have an old-fashioned CEO who would never agree to my proposal. He would start rationalizing or playing games. I thought a long time about how to go about it, whether I should try, and what would happen if I did. I ended up doing nothing, doing my usual work in my usual way."

Chris: "My colleague said, 'People in the business say bad things about you, but I won't say who — that wouldn't be fair to them.' I saw what he meant, but I retreated to reason. I started turning the situation over and over in my mind. Then I became really emotional and before long I started thinking again, then became emotional again, and went back and forth between the two extremes. At the end of the week I got tired of not being able to do anything about the situation. It drove me away from my people. It scared me that they talked about me behind my back. I even struggled with apathy. My wife said, 'Don't think about it anymore and don't feel bad about it. Just drop it.'"

The Courage to Connect

If you want to reach your goals and achieve your dreams, break-through is bound to occur. But your reason and emotions and other safe internal mechanisms may keep you from reaching your goals and making your dreams come true. Defense mechanisms may

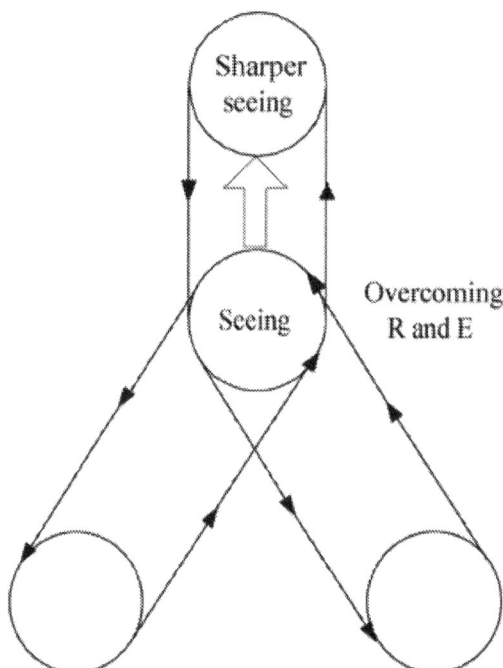

destroy your first moments of seeing and intuition so that you are unable to come to sharper seeing.

Remember Copernicus and his challenge to the idea of a flat Earth? Because of your discomfort, you seek refuge by thinking in terms of a flat Earth: "I can't do it, I don't have the courage, I don't know how," you tell yourself. You lose interest in your goals. And, almost imperceptibly, you relapse and use only your rational or emotional side again. You can even bounce back and forth between R and E without seeing anymore, imbalanced. After awhile, as an expression of a kind of exhaustion, you sink into apathy. You slip back into your old behavior patterns.

So the question remains: Do you want to break the rules?

If so, you need the Courage to Connect — the courage to integrate your thoughts and actions and face the barriers and tensions. Face your discomfort — do not run away from it to your favored E or R side or apathy. Use it to connect your reason with your emotions. You have no choice but to believe in a round Earth and take your first steps into the unknown.

Overcoming Conflict and Barriers: Mindset Change

If you do overcome conflict and barriers, it leads to the integration of your basic capacities, R and E, and even to new capacities: seeing and even further development of your self or ego through the process of seeing more and more.

Seeing: The Eureka! Moment

When you see things clearly, then you have come to an integration of your R and E sides. If you don't see clearly, you didn't make a successful integration. In abstract terms: either you "see" the mathematical formula of Pythagoras — $a^2 + b^2 = c^2$ — or you don't.

If people experience a barrier in understanding this formula, they retreat to either their reason or their emotions. In the first case they may ask themselves, "What, for heaven's sake, is the character a?" In the second case they might throw away the book and say, "What do I need mathematics for? I don't want to learn this formula." But when you actually see it, you're thinking fast and feeling it at the same time. Your fast thinking and feelings stick together — they integrate — which results in insight or seeing. Eureka!

The Pitfalls of Seeing

Seeing, the so-called eureka experience, is not free of pitfalls. What can happen? Let's take a look at Otto:

Example 1: Seeing Can Be Fleeting

Otto (31, promotion manager of an insurance company) is brooding on certain solutions and just achieved a moment of seeing. Just then his colleague asks him if he wants a cup of coffee, and boom — the moment of seeing is gone. Sometimes this moment returns quickly, but occasionally it can take quite some time before he'll have the same insight again. His "eureka" moment is gone, since "eureka" is vulnerable, fragile, and small, often even lighter then the touch of a feather.

Otto's experience gives rise to another important insight: although he himself might be capable of coming to seeing, his environment can prevent him from making the most of his eureka experience. Other people, especially, can distract us from seeing if they don't share our vision.

Example 2: The Excitement of Seeing Can Be Overwhelming

After a long time of hard work and research, Chris knows precisely what to say in his report. Eureka, he sees it. This seeing causes him so much excitement and tension that he fails to achieve anything else for the rest of the week. In fact, he doesn't even work on his report so that he doesn't upset his dream.

In Chris's example, we can see that even in a few seconds he can swerve from seeing clearly to exhaustion and apathy. Just as the ball thrown into the air will fall because of gravity, he can experience a force that pulls him down. It will take him days to act on his eureka moment.

Example 3: Distractions Can Delay or Prevent Seeing

Bill notices that his colleague's workspace is messy and projects a terrible image. Bill wants something to be done about it. His colleague, seeing that Bill is upset about it, asks about a meeting yesterday that didn't go well. Bill discusses it and then forgets to express his irritation about the mess.

There are many ways in which you can be prevented from seeing things. You may be caught off guard by questions or remarks. You may be asked about your vacation in order to camouflage the inferior quality of a delivered report. Events like these can keep you from having eureka moments. Additionally, other people can push you back into reason or emotion. Then you can get stuck bouncing back and forth between R and E, without seeing anymore, and even retreat to a point of apathy.

Example 4: Seeing Can Be Like a Roller Coaster

When Jane sees that the other units' actions will hinder her progress, she gets frustrated. They take action without her while saying they need her input. She sees it's becoming an "us versus them" story and it's sucking up a lot of her energy and time. She feels uncomfortable and starts reasoning that she can't influence them because they are the owners of the project. And when they aren't committed to sharing ownership, she can't guarantee that she'll meet her deadline. She feels bad about this and is even becoming depressed.

If and when Jane grabs the tension and discomfort like a football, she will be able to do something about her uncomfortable situation. Nevertheless, her tension has a function. The trick is to stop thinking of this tension as a factor for delay and, rather, think about it as an opportunity for seeing. It's like being on a roller coaster. The roller coaster travels at a certain speed in a certain direction. Suddenly the roller coaster speeds down a hill and then up a hill just as unexpectedly. This loop of the track is where the roller coaster gains momentum.

So Jane can actively pay attention to her problems with the project: the ownership issue, and her team's lack of commitment. Then she can actively direct her negative thoughts and bad feelings — the downhill movement — to an upward course again. So by focusing she can change the direction of her feelings — from going downhill to going up again. That is the way acceleration and momentum are achieved.

Exercise: Creating Acceleration and Momentum

In this exercise, you'll learn how to change direction on your R-and-E roller coaster and create acceleration and momentum. Answer the following questions and note where they appear in the cycle:

1. What is your biggest problem?
2. Why can't you do anything about it?
3. How can you solve it and take ownership?

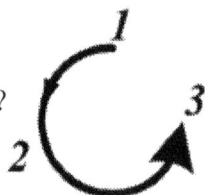

The Power of Seeing: Successful Integration

If you want to use the power of seeing, you will have to develop strength to sustain it and develop it even further toward foresight. You must continuously try to overcome your own discomfort and barriers as well as protect your moments of insight from the experience of discomfort and barriers presented by others. Other people can push you with their R or E into your R or E and can even use their apathy to move you into your R, E, or apathy. But if you succeed in gaining power over your eureka moments, you will be able to break into new layers of seeing, helping you to see more and more. Breaking through the barriers and discomfort can become transformational. You can start behaving differently and see more. The roller coaster experiences are the expressions of the process of your inner growth.

If you're experiencing great discomfort, don't:

- Seek more facts, make too many spreadsheets
- Distract others and make them insecure by keeping them from working

- Run away from the problem
- Find someone to project your own problems onto

Exercise: Your Twenty-Nine-Second Task

To overcome great discomfort, do one of these twenty-nine-second exercises:

- Take a cardboard box and write on each side, listing everything you are afraid of, nervous about, and fed up with. Then take a baseball bat and bash it. Or take a piece of paper and write down all your discomforts. Ball the paper up and throw it against the wall (or in the wastebasket if you do not want scare someone). You can also burn it, but please do this safely or outside.
- Take the focus: What do you want to achieve? Why will you fail? Why will you succeed?
- Or write down: What is the matter? Why is this a problem? Why isn't this a problem?
- Close your eyes. Imagine openly and freely telling the person you are frustrated with what you think about him or her. Then imagine that you make up. Look for a shared focus and write it down.
- Look for the discomfort of the other person(s) and write down three ways that you could lead them through their discomfort.

Breaking Through the Barriers:
The Dream Agenda: The Power of Seeing

In the next diagram, you will find the Dream Agenda, a tool that helps you connect your logic and emotions, develop your seeing, and reach your dreams.

Dream Agenda: dream big, start small
Power of Seeing Agenda
Please fill in as follows: go from 1 to 1A, to 1B, to 2, to 2A, etc.

1. What are your dreams on the subject?
1.
2.
3.
4.

1A. Four reasons it will fail:
1.
2.
3.
4.

1B. Four reasons it will succeed:
1.
2.
3.
4.

2. What are your goals regarding the subject?
1.
2.
3.
4.

2A. Four reasons it will fail:
1.
2.
3.
4.

2B. Four reasons it will succeed:
1.
2.
3.
4.

3. What has to be arranged for the subject?
1.
2.
3.
4.

3A. Four reasons it will fail:
1.
2.
3.
4.

3B. Four reasons it will succeed:
1.
2.
3.
4.

4. What is the right logic toward the subject?
1.
2.
3.
4.

5. What is the right emotion toward the subject?
1.
2.
3.
4.

6. How can you avoid apathy toward the subject?
1.
2.
3.
4.

The Dream Agenda tool consists of a few questions. Take your time and write down the answers to the questions in the order in which they are presented. Every question is equally important. You can complete it by yourself by writing down the answers. To get maximum results, and to push yourself a little harder, have a friend ask you the questions. Afterwards you may swap and have your friend answer the questions. In both cases, you may write down the answers without speaking.

To use the Dream Agenda, start with a dream or goal, something you want to achieve. Take your time to answer these questions and be as honest as possible. Carefully note your reasons for why things will not work. These are emotions or rationalizations that will keep you from reaching your dream. Sometimes, people or situations may make you feel uncomfortable. Identifying them and asking yourself why and how they make you feel uncomfortable can help you overcome many barriers.

An Example: Where the Dream Agenda Could Help

Imagine the following situation.

You have set the goal of making a difficult phone call — you have to ask Gerald to rewrite a report for you. In all likelihood, he will be quite unhappy with your request. You get nervous and would rather not ask him.

Your R will provide you with reasons to avoid this unpleasant experience: "I don't want to call him. He's so assertive he'll probably refuse to help. How can I handle this?"

You feel terrible. You return to reason. If the job won't get done you must do it yourself. However, you don't have time to do it and you lack some insight in the issue. Besides, you're the boss, not Gerald.

You feel some frustration. "Oh, for Pete's sake . . ." you say to no one in particular.

Eventually, you feel apathetic and don't ask Gerald to rewrite the report. You don't think about it anymore and stop worrying. Your colleague Susan tells you to forget about it and move on.

The point is, (1) You can do it yourself, but you have little knowledge about the subject. (2) Susan's response leads you to rationalize the situation. Then (3) you feel terrible again. (4) In the end you decide to postpone the phone call until tomorrow.

Example:
Tension over a difficult telephone conversation

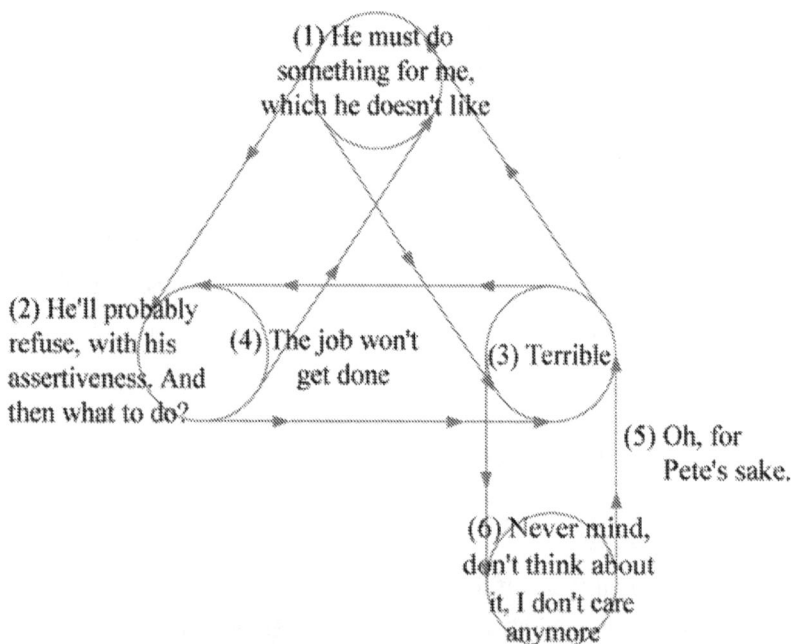

(1) He must do something for me, which he doesn't like

(2) He'll probably refuse, with his assertiveness. And then what to do?

(4) The job won't get done

(3) Terrible

(5) Oh, for Pete's sake.

(6) Never mind, don't think about it, I don't care anymore

Susan

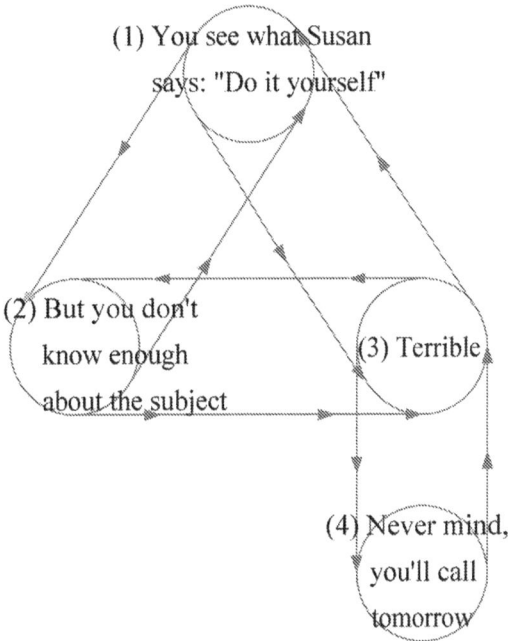

(1) You see what Susan says: "Do it yourself"

(2) But you don't know enough about the subject

(3) Terrible

(4) Never mind, you'll call tomorrow

How Can You Overcome and Reach Your Goal?

Your preparation might look like this:

1. You start by writing down your goal and by visualizing what you want to achieve. For example, your dream consists of having an improved version of the report with which you can convince your customer or build a better relationship. You need to ask Gerald to rewrite it.

2. Subsequently, you get stressed, experience discomfort, and hit a barrier.

3a. You note four reasons why you will not succeed in asking Gerald to write a better report for you. For example: (1) You are afraid to ask him, because he is always so assertive. (2) He will stop liking you. (3) You cannot summon the courage because you don't know how to frame your request. (4) You are afraid he will notice your insecurity.

3b. When you look at your answers, recognize the negativity emanating from them. You have written negative reasons that reflect your negative feelings.

4a. Try to replace negative reasons with positive ones by writing down four reasons why you will succeed: (1) You can put your request in very friendly terms. (2) You are confident he will still like you if you ask him to rewrite the report. (3) If he refuses, the two of you can talk about it. You can make him understand how important this is for you and eventually come to shared ownership. (4) The report needs to be finished.

4b. Positive feelings occur.

5. Your last action is to pick up the phone and start calling.

Preparation for a phone call

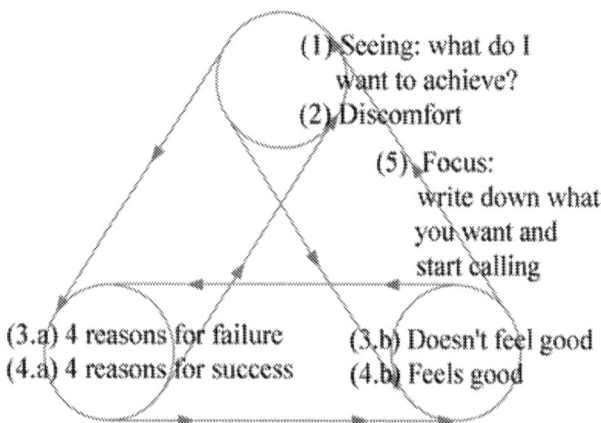

(1) Seeing: what do I want to achieve?
(2) Discomfort
(5) Focus: write down what you want and start calling
(3.a) 4 reasons for failure
(4.a) 4 reasons for success
(3.b) Doesn't feel good
(4.b) Feels good

The Heart of The Courage to Connect

Is that all there is to it? Yes, it really is this simple. You will see for yourself that it works. Just make sure you maintain the discipline of formulating your focus, dreams, and goals and continue using the tool.

In short:

(1) What do you want?
(2) Why is what you want a problem?
(3) Why isn't it a problem?

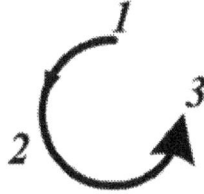

The Dream Agenda: The Power of Seeing

We will now introduce this tool step by step so that you have a detailed view of what goes into creating your Dream Agenda.

Dreams

Start by describing your dream. This may be a dream you feel very strongly about, but you can also think of more modest dreams. You may want to close a deal, you may want to discuss a merger with your colleague, or you may want to improve your relationship with your partner. Exploring your dream makes you more powerful.

Four Reasons Why You Will Fail and Why You Will Succeed

By writing down reasons why you will fail and why you will succeed, you will be pushed beyond your discomfort and into a positive state of mind. By explicitly stating why something will fail or succeed, you connect your reason with your emotion.

What if a reason is so powerful that you cannot dismiss it by simply turning to your positive feelings? In such a case, you should take some time and formulate a dream around the problem.

For example, one reason why you are convinced that your deal will fail is that you can't stand the bank manager. In such a case, you may develop a new Dream Agenda centered on a better relationship with the bank manager. By taking this extra step, you can solve the problem.

Goals

By writing down your goals, you are forced to be a bit more concrete about what you have to do to accomplish your dream. Use your seeing to lead you to the goals. It is not easy to be specific about all the steps you need to take, but by simply making the effort, you will get closer to your dream and have a clearer view of where to go.

Four Reasons Why You Will or Will Not Succeed

Just as in the case of your dreams, you may experience discomfort in thinking about how to achieve your goals. Again, it is a matter of barriers. Use the questions in the same way you did with your dreams. If there is an answer to a "why not" question that is bothering you, you may try to solve it at the next level, under "things that have to be done."

Things That Have to Be Done

Some of the things that have to be done require only minor actions. These preparations can be very simple; you just need to have the discipline to proceed. When you dream big you have to start small, step by step, to get from where you are to where you want to be.

Four Reasons Why This Will or Will Not Succeed

The reasons why you think that something will not succeed are often, even at this practical level of planning things, quite trivial. Such reasons may include a lack of time, initial hesitation, or a phone call that has to be made. Remember that each aspect, however trivial, is part of your dream and deserves the same amount of attention as the reasons you provided at a higher level.

Do's and Don'ts in Handling Discomfort and Using the Dream Agenda

The following dos and don'ts may help you feel a bit more at ease with discomfort.

Don't:

- Reason endlessly
- Worry
- Think in circles
- Act impulsively

Do:

- Keep up your courage
- Use the exercises (frequently)
- Keep an eye on your dreams
- Address your discomfort

Once you start using the Dream Agenda, you may well get addicted to it. In the fifth chapter we will talk about gearing up for success. You will learn how to internalize the courage to connect and make it your own.

Accelerating Success: Doing Things Differently

Building Self-Confidence

Once you start working with the Dream Agenda, you may find the reasons you mentioned for not achieving your goals to be quite trivial.

Jane: "When I started working with the model, I dreaded writing down the four reasons why I would not be able to reach my goal. I felt silly and embarrassed. Each time I could think of only two reasons, and those were so trivial!"

It is precisely such triviality that will inspire confidence. After all, if these are the only reasons that keep you from achieving your goals, you might as well be convinced by the potential for success.

Your four reasons for failure force you to connect with your negative feelings and modes of reasoning. Initially, this may have a negative impact on your self-image. However, as you replace negative feelings with positive ones, you will gradually boost your self-esteem.

Gloria (29, owner of a florist shop): "When I was writing down the four reasons things wouldn't work, I always included one reason such as: 'I am not smart enough' or 'I am not strong enough.' But now I know that such doubt will be followed by one of the four reasons that things will work: 'I AM strong enough. I CAN make it work.'"

Obviously, your self-esteem will continue to be reinforced as you achieve your goals and dreams and are carried forward by the momentum you have created yourself.

How to Use the Dream Agenda: The Power of Seeing

It is not necessary to discuss the reasons that you list with other people. It is an internal process. The important thing is to clarify the four reasons for yourself.

Valerie (49, company physician): "Writing down the four reasons for failure in perfect silence has always been a powerful exercise for me. Just stating the reasons on paper and make them explicit acts as a motivating challenge: 'I am going to do this. Why should I hesitate?'"

Enjoying Life

Once you start using the tool, you will find that life becomes more exciting. After your first success, you will want to use the Dream Agenda more and more. You may experience a sense of freedom, as Peter does.

Peter (52, design firm director): "I try not to take things too seriously anymore. I have decided to do only the things I really want to from now on. Using the exercises, I can make my dreams come true and enjoy what I do and enjoy helping others with it. So why shouldn't I do it?"

This sense of freedom develops as your courage increases. The Dream Agenda inspires such courage. You begin to feel increasingly confident about your actions and the goals you want to achieve. You may even start experimenting with different solutions that depart from your normal, predictable way of doing things.

Hans (58, sales director of a food company): "I had a session with my team leaders. Everything went exactly as planned. But after the meeting, everyone felt dissatisfied. 'Why not let go of the agenda and the slides for the next round of meetings?' I said to myself. I prepared myself mentally and gave it a try. It was a very uncomfortable experience for all of us but an eye-opener at the same time. We made our fears explicit, which was a tremendously big step. It was the best meeting we'd had in a long time."

Actively Looking for Discomfort

Once you start using the Dream Agenda, you will become more successful. As you become increasingly aware of your discomfort and barriers to growth, these barriers will be removed. The first time that you address difficult issues with your team may be a frightening experience. But the second time will be easier, and after awhile it will become a habit. Eventually, you will find that your next barrier lies farther away and doesn't seem so daunting. You will continue to move forward, accelerating the process.

Sonia (34, sales services manager): "At first I felt a bit silly writing down why something wouldn't work and why it would. But now as I go through this process every day, I have come to know myself better. I know what I have to do to take a step forward. In fact, I move a bit farther every time, because what used to feel uncomfortable the

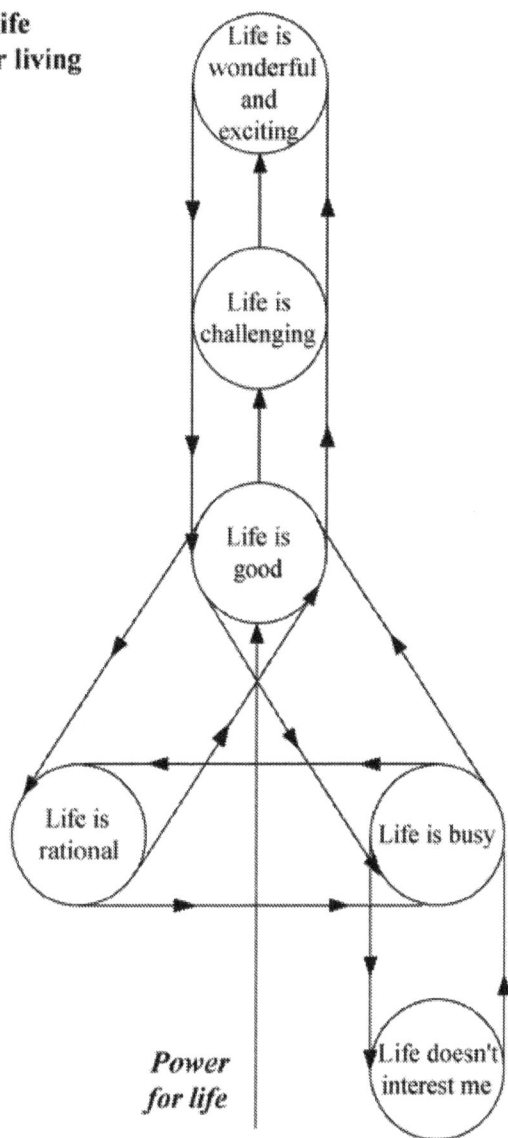

Enjoying life
Passion for living

Life is
wonderful
and
exciting

Life is
challenging

Life is
good

Life is
rational

Life is busy

Power
for life

Life doesn't
interest me

*first time becomes comfortable after some practice. I look forward
to my next dream already. I want to learn what top leaders do."*

Your success also increases because of your preparation, which
makes you focus on what you want to achieve. In all kinds of different situations, you will start thinking about goals, dreams, and
reasons for failure and success.

*Simone (39, account manager): "Now that I know that the tool works,
I prepare myself better for all kinds of situations: meetings with my
staff, discussions with my colleagues, and even conversations with my
partner. I make a point of taking the time to make my goals explicit
and asking myself the questions about failure and success."*

Gearing up for success means that instead of waiting for your discomfort to appear, you actively start
looking for it. You start to explore your own barriers by discovering where the discomfort begins.
In doing so, you begin to develop yourself.

ego

This diagram shows the way the
roller coaster travels at a certain speed
in a certain direction. When the R and
E are successfully connected the

ego

"aha" moment occurs when you
snap your fingers and suddenly
"see it!" This inner self-aware-
ness is the ego, which sits in

ego

the roller-coaster situation.
Remember the focus, the fail-
succeed exercises we

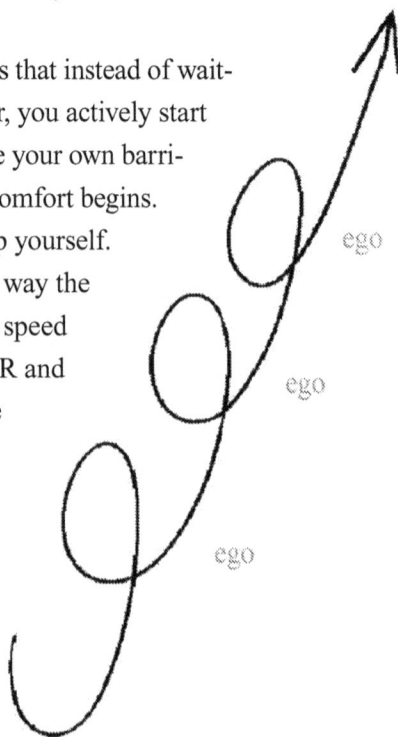

mentioned previously. In this diagram the ego is in a continuous process of seeing more clearly all the time, step by step, accelerating forward.

Remember the issues that were on the agenda in Chapter One:

- Gearing up for success
- Breaking through your barriers: stretching expectations of yourself and others
- Trying to change the mindset of people around you
- Creating an energizing vision
- Coaching and mentoring others to accelerate their development
- Bringing team conflict out into the open in order to resolve it

When you first picked up this book, you probably had no clue about how to deal with these issues. But now you have the tools and with your new eagerness to look for discomfort, you will deal with these issues one by one. And better yet, you will succeed!

Overcoming the tension and barriers of connecting

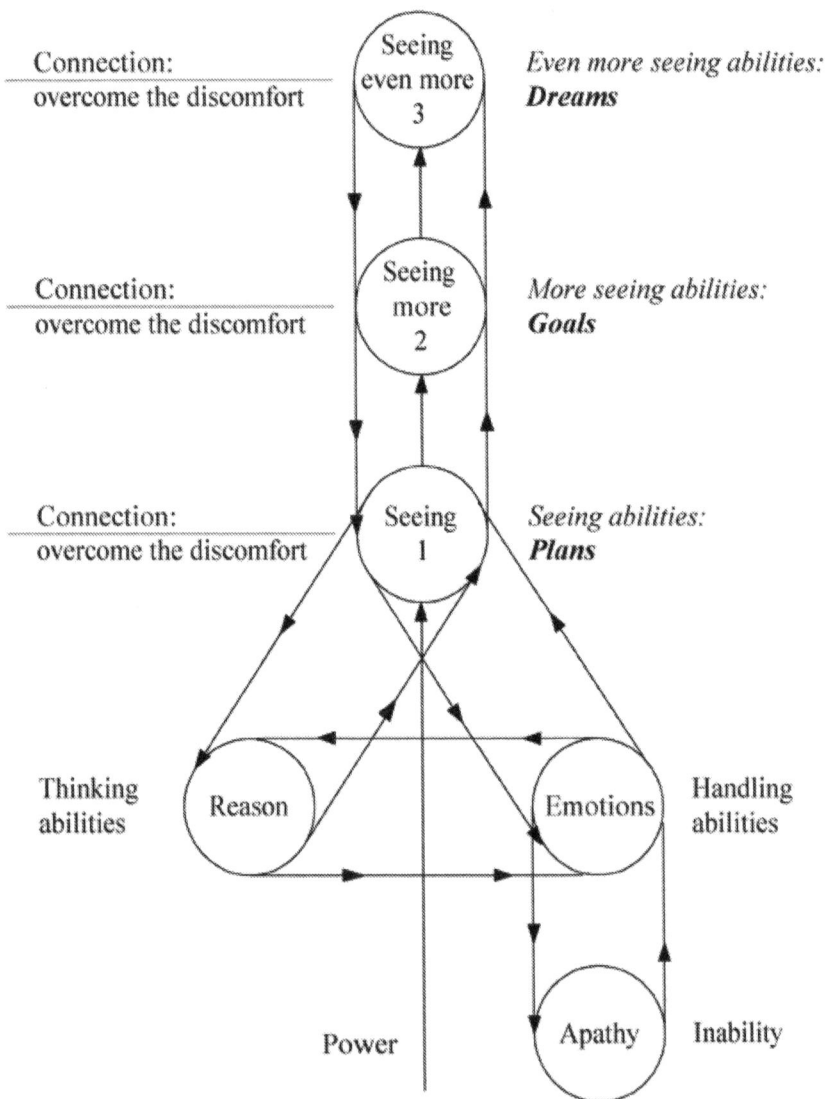

Connection:
overcome the discomfort

Seeing
even more
3

Even more seeing abilities:
Dreams

Connection:
overcome the discomfort

Seeing
more
2

More seeing abilities:
Goals

Connection:
overcome the discomfort

Seeing
1

Seeing abilities:
Plans

Thinking
abilities

Reason

Emotions

Handling
abilities

Power

Apathy

Inability

CHAPTER 6:

The Courage to Overcome in Business

In this chapter you will get a view of how the Courage to Connect model fits with leading others, the organization and the company as a whole. You will also get a taste of how to expand upon these ideas, including how to tackle the issue of leading a company as an integration of leading the people (emotional issues) and the organization (reason issues).

The issues:

- Dealing with the tension and barriers coming from the connection between R and E and overcoming the barriers and the tension of differences between consumers, shareholders, yourself and others, other teams, other units, the organization, the company and the market, other disciplines, and other interests. (Dealing with these issues is in fact a reconnecting activity.)
- Dealing with the tension of integration (bringing things together in order to solve a problem) versus fragmentation (focusing on the individual parts without considering the big picture); of innovation versus structure, organization, and day-to-day business.
- Learning to deal with the tension of connecting hard and soft issues in business.
- Learning to focus and behave differently.

- Focusing on clear dreams and strategy, then implementing these in the organization while staying on course and remaining flexible enough to deal with the tension of unexpected events.

With the Courage to Connect you can form your dream and develop clear strategy for the company (or at least your part of it) and integrate these with the organization, the people, and actions.

It is of great importance to make use of the tension among units, management, and employees for the transformation of all. You can use this discomfort and barriers to steer through hard and soft issues within and outside of the company. Otherwise you may fall too often into game playing and compromising to reduce the tension.

Newton's Law and Overcoming Tension

When we actively connect our seeing experience with the tensions involved, we engage in a process similar to Newton's Law: Power (F) = Seeing (M) x Tension (A). When seeing and tension collide, force (an acceleration to see more) occurs. Powerful insight comes from actively using the barriers and tension from seeing.

Passion is extinguished when there is no tension left. When a man or woman agrees with his or her partner to avoid tension, then there is no energy left in the relationship. The possibility exists that there is no passion left, either.

Self-leadership

In this book you have seen how to gain control and lead the inner growth process of the ego, which we call self-leadership. This also forms the basis of the steps you might have to take when leading

Overcoming the tension of connecting

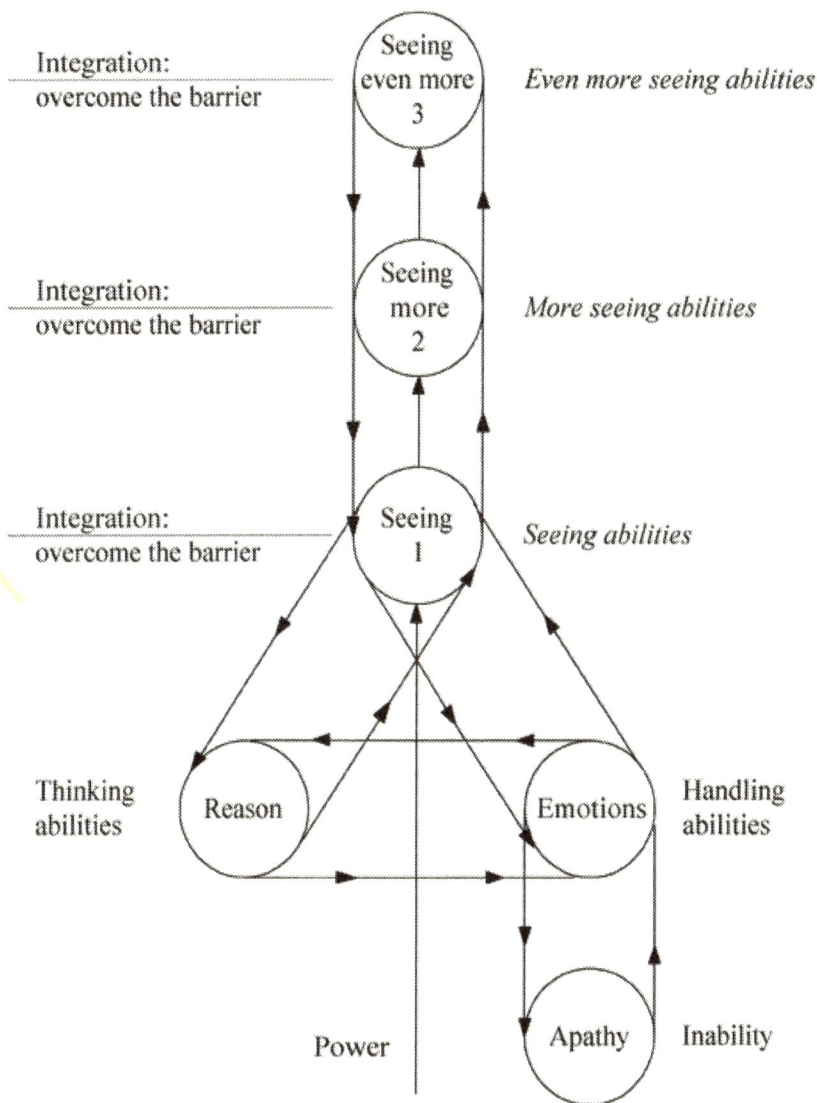

Integration:
overcome the barrier

Seeing
even more
3

Even more seeing abilities

Integration:
overcome the barrier

Seeing
more
2

More seeing abilities

Integration:
overcome the barrier

Seeing
1

Seeing abilities

Thinking
abilities

Reason

Emotions

Handling
abilities

Power

Apathy

Inability

others or leading the organization and integrating the people with the organization. This inner growth process may even advance your career.

Toward Top Leadership

If you work through your own discomfort and tension, which can oftentimes feel like a roller-coaster experience, and continue to successfully integrate your R and E you will come to a deeper level of insight and ultimately foresight. If you dare to take ownership of your own issues and possible problems, then you develop leadership. The first step of this process can be described as coming to ownership. In general this process can be illustrated by a little roller-coaster visual and a twenty-nine-second exercise.

Exercise: Creating Ownership

Following the points in the cycle illustrated in the diagram, write down the answers to these three questions:
(1) What is your biggest problem?
(2) Why can't you do anything about it?
(3) How can you solve it and create ownership?

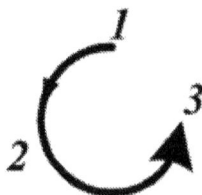

Phases of Leadership

In a successful integration of R and E, three distinct phases of leadership can be distinguished: manager, leader, and top leader. These three phases represent the different levels of seeing and guiding needed to obtain further insight. This can be described as the state in which the seeing has anchored itself and does not disappear easily. It can be said that the manager settles things via ownership, the leader reaches his goals via his vision, and the top leader makes dreams come true by way of his beliefs.

Management and Ownership:
The First Step of Successful Integration

In this first step a leader has overcome the tension of seeing problems and challenges or possible solutions. He or she dares to take ownership of the issues. At this point managers can even take the steps to achieve their goals. In short, the management level represents the ability to arrange things.

Leadership and Vision: The Next Step of Integration

In this second step a leader has developed the ability to attain long-term goals by successfully embracing the tension of seeing, which speeds up — instead of slows down — the realization of his dreams. In short, this leadership level represents the ability to achieve goals.

Top Leadership and Belief:
The Next Phase of Integration

In this phase, differences between people and in the organization are tackled. An even greater speed of productive working and decision-making is seen. The top leader can form a belief and lead the integration of hard and soft issues within the company (or within a part of it) and its people.

In a true top leader we can find the ability to achieve the impossible.

To be in charge one must have power. You can get this power by connecting your seeing with tension. The stronger the barriers are, the stronger this power can be. Be mindful that the tension can delay the acceleration and progress toward your dream, but with your inner strength you can embrace the tension, and with your focus you can give your power its direction. What you see, the insight you gain, is dependent on your R and E. If one of them is ruling the other, you can be diverted or distracted and your inner resolve is weakened.

Leading Others

The diagram on the following page shows what happens if you enter the different levels of leadership. From being extremely busy and thinking about things over and over again, you move on to planning things, achieving goals, and making dreams come true. With others you are able to come to shared ownership, shared vision, and shared beliefs, because you have helped your colleagues overcome their own tension, discomfort, and barriers.

Leading the Organization

At the organizational level you can start integrating hard and soft issues, operations, and policy into the tactical, strategic, and entre-preneurial levels.

Leading a part of a company or an entire one — or even leading yourself — can be difficult. Even if you know what you want and have a clear strategy, you need to connect with the company. Yet this is often difficult to achieve when the lower organizational levels become involved. As you may know, transformation and acceleration require a certain pace. It is therefore important to get speed, power, and focus into this process. Above all, the process is personal: everyone has to go through the transformation themselves. Managers, for example, can't shove the responsibility for transformation onto others such as employees or consultants. Instead, they discover that it is

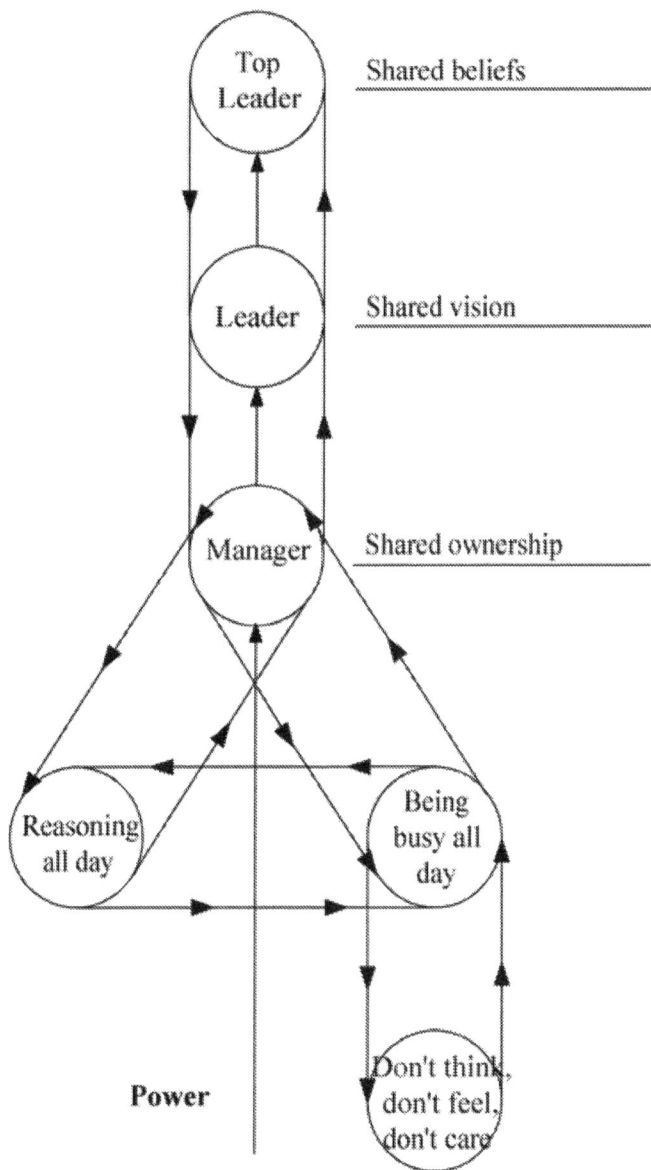

Top
Leader

Shared beliefs

Leader

Shared vision

Manager

Shared ownership

Reasoning
all day

Being
busy all
day

Don't think,
don't feel,
don't care

Power

Leading the Organization

Levels in organizations
Super-integrated levels

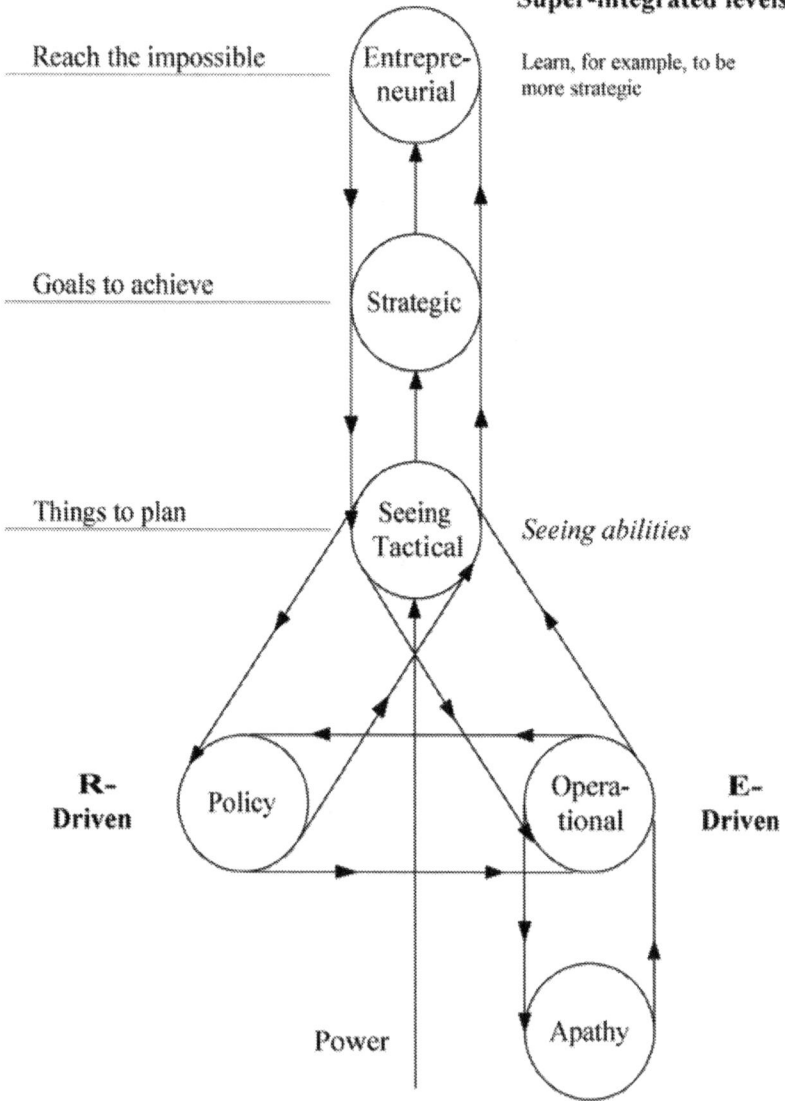

Reach the impossible

Entrepre-neurial

Learn, for example, to be more strategic

Goals to achieve

Strategic

Things to plan

Seeing Tactical

Seeing abilities

R-Driven

Policy

Opera-tional

E-Driven

Power

Apathy

easier and more fun to try to do things differently themselves.

Organizations, of course, keep moving and transforming; happily this is both explainable and executable. In contrast, an approach that is just one-dimensional actually requires more time and energy on the part of the leader.

An approach with a transformational element is needed. For fifteen years we have been working with the Courage to Connect model in large companies, and we've witnessed a number of transformations.

The Entrepreneur and the Courage to Connect

A top leader who is also an entrepreneur does not have a static position. Even at this level it is possible to grow more by continuously accepting barriers, tensions, and discomfort. At this level its unlikely that a person will relapse to R and E. Think about the following questions: Will an entrepreneur get stuck in his or her thoughts and not act? Will a real entrepreneur be busy without producing something tangible or important?

These questions should be answered negatively. At the top level of business, the entrepreneur will follow his intuitive signals, which require a slight bit of energy. It's about the spark. The rest of the time he or she is figuring out what he or she saw at the moment of inspiration, or seeing, and is trying to move and inspire others with their passion. The lightning insight — the "aha," the flash, the eureka moment — happens suddenly and all at once. Some important entrepreneurs with forceful insights don't accept any dissent — it is "their way or the highway." But in fact, seeing is a kind of clairvoyance — the culmination of fast thinking totally integrated with feeling — and this moves employees forward in the right direction.

The sharpest seeing is also designed and presented very clearly and persuasively. The tension belonging to the "aha" moment is overcome and used to create an increased focus on the desired result.

It Doesn't Begin Until You're There

Together, all of us create the organization, and the organization tells us to do this and do that. This leads to differentiation, a centrifugal movement that naturally splits things apart.

In contrast, think about the sensation you get when things fit and everything comes together, like when all of the people you love are at the same party. It just fits and feels right. That is what happens when the human being and the organization come together — they fit. Seeing-driven leadership, in contrast to traditional organizational leadership, brings together ideas, perspectives, and people and enables us to overcome differences, the organization paradox, and the cognitive dissonance within people. Leading the company is a real possibility when it's driven by seeing. Such leadership positively impacts the organization (hard issues) and the people (soft issues) working in it, so that the hard and soft issues are integrated at every level, into every fiber and every opinion. When the leadership and integration stick together, it is possible to gear up for the next connection of hard and soft issues.

About Top Leadership, Entrepreneurship, and Global Responsibility

In the beginning of our work, we help leaders develop self-leadership and entrepreneurship and connect their inner selves. Subsequently, they learn to make the connection with their surroundings and company and also deal with problems outside their company. When we help companies achieve greater success, we can also help them to prove their leadership by addressing world problems such as safety, the environment, poverty, and discrimination.

Let's take care of each other, helping the rational and the emotional sides come to clear, shared strategic action. Very often decisions are made on the basis of one's perception of reality. Doesn't it make sense that those with the clearest view of reality are also able to make the best decisions?

The Next Step

The approach of this book shows the entrepreneurial capacities of people on an individual level. It helps individuals overcome the inner tension between reason and emotion and uses this tension to speed up growth. The next step addresses the organization and the people as a whole. It also describes the development of teams, the company, and the business.

Thank you for your attention. We wish you inner and outer connection, happiness, and, in the end, love.

If you would like to know more about the Courage to Connect model, please visit our website at www.couragetoconnect.com.

Frequently Asked Questions

How Do I Integrate My Reason and My Emotions?

If you feel you are not succeeding in integrating your reason and your emotions, you may want to try the following exercise. Think of yourself in a common situation such as a meeting, a sales transaction, or a telephone call. Try to describe your own behavior according to the different examples provided in Chapter Two. If, for example, you turn out to be too rationally oriented, introduce one emotional aspect the next time you find yourself in such a situation. For example, look at a flower, a picture, or a person. Then get focused again. Ask yourself why you have to use reason in this situation. Next, ask yourself why you don't need to do that. In doing so, you will gradually learn to integrate rationally convincing and emotionally appealing behavior.

When you are too emotional and want to react impulsively, in your mind, run into a meadow and mow all the grass and then refocus again. Or, alternatively, imagine a very thick tree trunk and saw it in half as fast as you can. Then focus again on what you want.

When you experience tension or some anxiety from the integration of R and E, try writing down your discomfort on a piece of paper and then throw it in a wastebasket or tear it apart. If you can't do that, at least imagine doing so. Perhaps you can imagine blowing your discomfort into a balloon and letting the wind take it into the air. Re-focus again.

How Can I Define My Dream?

Many people have difficulty defining their dreams. Keep in mind that a dream can exist at different levels and can be about different ambitions. Dreams do not have to be about material success; dreams about aging well and staying healthy and happy are valid. You can have more than one dream, and your dreams can be big or small.

To develop your dreams you need to take a closer look at yourself. What do you want right now? What do you want to achieve in the next ten years? In addition, defining your dream requires an environment in which you will not be disturbed. Find a spot where you feel comfortable and start thinking about what you have always wanted to do.

Why Must I Proceed Step by Step?

Let's compare the seeing approach with driving a car. The apathetic stage is the empty tank situation. The emotion is the engine. The reason is the steering and the wheels. The clutch is the integration. In order to reach a high speed, you must shift to a higher gear.

That's much like the transformation process and the repeated integration of reason and emotion. It has to be done step by step. You are not allowed to skip steps but you can go very fast within the steps. Doing so results in smooth shifting. Otherwise, you can blow up the engine and won't be able to move and focus anymore. Please note you are both driver and car at the same time.

Visual: Courage as a car on the highway

Compare the seeing approach to a car. By linking the motor (=drive) and a steering-wheel (=giving direction) together, you are going ahead. After shifting to higher gears you obtain maximum speed. To get smooth gear-shifting you have to go step-by-step.

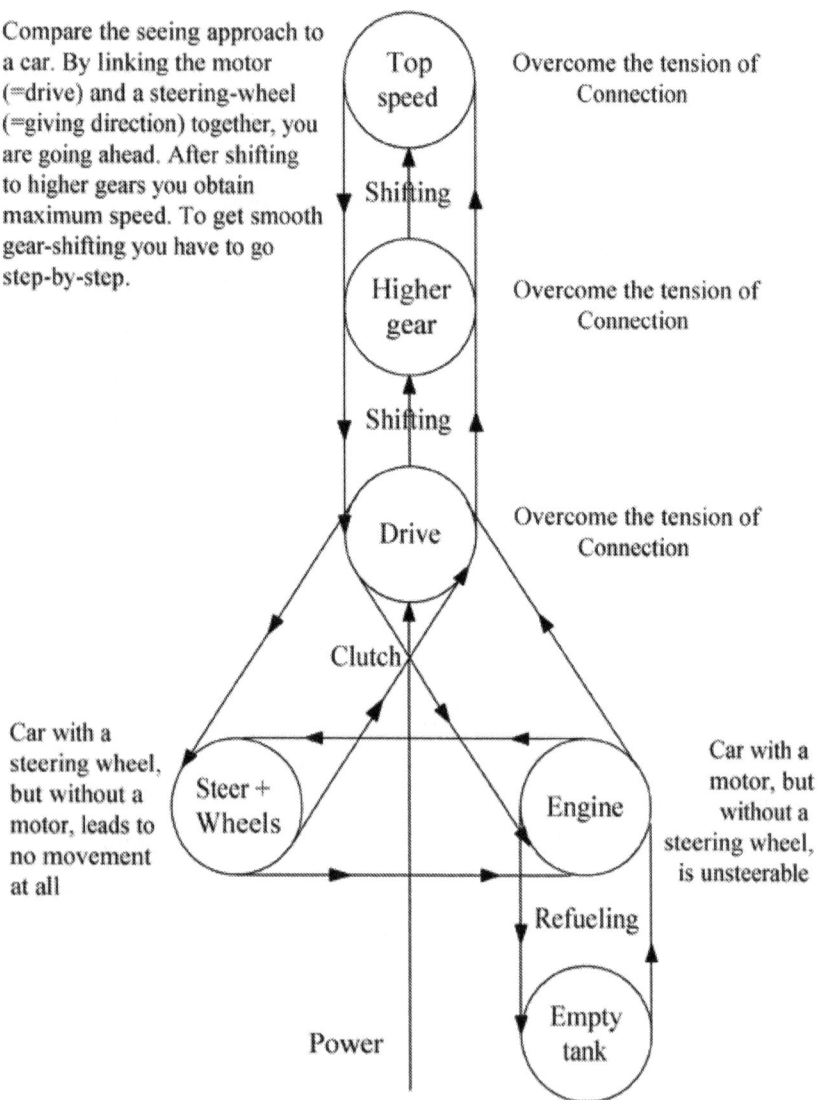

Top speed

Overcome the tension of Connection

Shifting

Higher gear

Overcome the tension of Connection

Shifting

Drive

Overcome the tension of Connection

Clutch

Car with a steering wheel, but without a motor, leads to no movement at all

Steer + Wheels

Engine

Car with a motor, but without a steering wheel, is unsteerable

Refueling

Power

Empty tank

How Can I Remain Honest with Myself?

Sometimes it is difficult to be honest and open with yourself. If this is the case, it can be useful to ask a good friend to keep reminding you of your intentions.

Why Should I Write Down Reasons Things Will Not Succeed?

Writing down why your plan will not succeed can be difficult. You may cling to the hope that everything will work out just fine so that you don't become discouraged. Sometimes it is even considered embarrassing to admit the possibility of failure. As we mentioned in Chapter Five, trivial things can have great impact — that is why it is important to commit your fears of failure to paper and then move forward with the reasons for success.

How Can I Make It Easier to Come Up With Reasons for Success?

When you are having difficulty noting the reasons for success, stop for a second and think of your greatest achievements. List your personal qualities that contributed to such achievements. After this, you will find it easier to proceed with the reasons for success.

How Do I Take Real Action After Completing the Dream Agenda?

When you have filled out the Dream Agenda, you will have drawn up a list of steps that need to be taken before a goal can be reached. If you find it difficult to stick to these steps, ask a friend to keep you on the right track; he or she can alert you when you aren't making progress. In addition, you can create a Dream Agenda addressing a particular prerequisite for a specific goal.

Where Can I Find More Information About the Courage to Connect?

Please visit our website at couragetoconnect.com to learn more about our methods and services.

Summary

Surpassing Reason and Emotion

People have two basic capacities: reason and emotion. At the moment we use these capacities together a new capacity arises, which we call "seeing." When "seeing" happens, thinking and feeling grab each other in a way to create moments of breakthrough thinking or insight. When we see something, we think quickly, feel it immediately, and in an instant know what we have to do. In such a situation a new awareness of one's self arises, an ego from which everything starts and decisions are made. That is what this book is about.

Tension from the Connection

Along with this seeing comes some discomfort. What we see, experience, or are aware of can create tension. Because of this tension we often return to what is comfortable — our reason, for example — and start thinking, reasoning, and puzzling over the situation, paralyzed by indecision, with slow and few actions. Alternately, the tension may lead us to retreat to our emotions. We may feel bad and, in an effort to rid ourselves of the uncomfortable feelings, may act impulsively. As a result, our decisions can often be thoughtless and may only Band-Aid the situation rather than provide a long-term solution. Without "seeing" between our thoughts and feelings, we can come home one day endlessly reasoning and the next day acting emotionally. This bouncing back and forth between reason and emotion can last awhile and be exhausting. The result is that you fall into apathy and fail to care anymore. Friends and partners will give you the same advice: get over it and don't think about it anymore.

The Tension of the Other

Sometimes when you do see, someone else may not agree or share your insight. Perhaps you are thought of as stupid and, in the worst case, crazy. This can push you back into your reasoning or emotions. As a result you may become apathetic, incapable of any action at all.

The Tension of Success

On the other hand, sometimes the excitement of seeing — for example, seeing that you just might be successful — can be overwhelming and immobilizing. It's as if you've reached the top of the mountain with your seeing and then are forced by gravity to slip down the slopes. You can retreat into reasoning or your emotions and this may eventually lead to apathy.

From Clear Strategy to Focused Action: Successfully Overcoming

In this book we talk about successfully handling the tension that belongs to overcoming reason and emotion in order to achieve seeing-driven behavior. This is the clear and plain insight about what must happen. The tension such insight gives is used to come to an even clearer vision of what is needed to progress to action. Eventually this process leads to a belief in your own capacities, a trust that what you see can bring you to strategically correct actions and solutions. You can share this vision, strategy, and belief with others, while also helping them to successfully overcome the tension they too experience from seeing.

Becoming Entrepreneurial

The road to becoming entrepreneurial starts with a firm base of seeing. Being able to successfully handle the tension of seeing ensures that strategies become obvious and clear.

Step-by-Step Progress, Timing, and Focus

Seeing and tackling problems that come to the surface can lead you to develop ownership of those problems. Continuing to see and focus makes possible the development of vision and belief in your solutions. By seeing, you arrive at the right steps, timing, focus, and order so that fears, barriers, and discomfort can be smashed and conquered. You tell yourself: "I have faith again, I see how to handle it, I see what to do and I just do it. I see how I can inspire people through this process."

Being Entrepreneurial and Achieving Self-leadership

Coming to seeing on your own means that you will achieve self-leadership, ownership of problems, and the ability to handle your problems by integrating your R and E sides. By doing so, you will avoid hesitation and endless information gathering (rationally driven behavior); impulsiveness, chaos, and weak short-term solutions (emotionally driven behavior); or walking away from the situation (apathy-driven behavior). Moving from ownership of problems to clear vision and insight, while dealing with your own discomfort, barriers, tensions, and possible fears, is a skill that can be built up step by step. You believe in your insight and agenda. This leads to handling what you stand for and going after what you truly believe — a personal or business dream, or a combination of both.

The Power of Insight

The approach in this book, *The Power of Insight,* reveals each person's entrepreneurial skills at an individual level. It helps them bridge the inner division between reason and emotion and uses the tension from this to develop entrepreneurship and accelerate the growth of entrepreneurship. With this tool the road to strategic action is described step by step. Central to this is seeing, the necessary and successful connection between our reason and our emotion, as a condition to come to a clear and shared strategy and a firm foundation of entrepreneurship.

About Strategy, Entrepreneurship, and Transformation

The Courage to Connect model creates a transformational moment — it leads to strategically shared action and possible entrepreneurship. In that sense the approach is descriptive, holistic, and sustainable rather than directive and normative. The Courage model uses tensions, discomfort, barriers, and possible fears about leaving one's comfort zone in order to arrive at a new experience of comfort. The approach uses the tension, discomfort, and barriers of connecting reason and emotion to gain insight, or the ability to see, in an easy and fun way so that one may get ahead. The approach also uses the moment of seeing and its tension to achieve action that is strategic, well timed, focused, and entrepreneurial.

The Future

This Is Just the Beginning!

We have conducted all kinds of research on the effects of the Courage to Connect model and related practical issues. More than 150,000 questionnaires based on our model have been filled out and processed by our sister company, Organizational Coaching. But more research is needed. We look to the latest findings by researchers like Antonio Damasio, the author of *The Feeling of What Happens*. These new discoveries show that the sense of self, the ego, is indeed near the brain's midline — where reason and emotion come together. These findings encourage us to continue in our own research.

Traditional science is often only rational and in that sense is one-dimensional. In *The Power of Insight,* transformation is the outcome of an integrated view of reason and emotions. Lists that tell managers what they should be — with terms like innovative, flexible, open, direct — will not lead to the desired transformation and will certainly not impact the levels of the organization with the greatest tensions and barriers. It is often difficult to transform higher and middle levels of management, and lists with thirty new rules and demands can be too much and too differentiated to work with.

We have fifteen years' worth of innovative approaches and solutions and are continuing to pioneer in all kind of ways. We're finding new methods to help leaders positively impact issues of safety, quality, the environment, and tensions in the community. The Courage to Connect model is a powerful approach that tries to make the unsolvable solvable. Our hope is to support leaders of the twenty-first century and secure our future. We believe in that future, in the power of love, in the power of overcoming and integrating hard and soft issues, as well as overcoming science (often R-driven) and business (often E-driven). We also believe in the power we have to handle the tension that comes from overcoming and building on this connection and achieving strategic actions with a soul. With a clear strategy, good order, right timing, and focus we can arrive at clear action with self-leadership and entrepreneurship.

Getting in Motion

Although human beings are incredibly complex, in some ways we are like a car. Our emotions are like the engine and our reason is like the steering wheel. By connecting these two we come to focused action. By shifting (or connecting our reason with our emotions) again and again, the car moves forward, but if the car has problems shifting it could overheat and ultimately break down. Likewise, we could become overwhelmed by the tension and become apathetic. In fact people are both driver and car in the same time. We are a super-integrated system of reason and emotions.

Inner Power

When we are authentically ourselves we are at our best. In fact, the greatest possible tension and fear we experience is the fear that we will change when reason and emotion come together. But integrated people can grow. The grown ego is strong and can achieve happiness and possibly even love. But isn't it possibly love, happiness, and even peace that create the tension that we're most afraid of? Isn't that the greatest paradox and challenge of the twenty-first century?

THIS BOOK IS A PARAVIEW SPECIAL EDITION

The imprint Paraview Special Editions focuses predominantly on publishing select out-of-print titles. Thanks to digital print-on-demand technology, it is easy and efficient to bring out-of-print titles back to life again, in essence making valuable books available to new audiences. Paraview Special Editions also publishes works of international authors and co-publishes projects with like-minded partner organizations, such as associations, magazines, and non-profit organizations. Other Paraview Special Editions and Paraview Press titles in responsible business include:

Corporate Renaissance   Rolf Österberg $14.95/£11.99
In this radical book on business and work, Swedish businessman Rolf Österberg argues that businesses have their priorities all wrong. Paradoxically, corporations also have the potential to act as an agent of change toward a human-oriented world. The solution lies in shifting our way of thinking and our perception of the world. This is Österberg's "new thought."

Leadership in a New Era   Edited by John Renesch $16.95/£12.99
This collection of vision and wisdom for tomorrow's business leaders is presented by a group of outstanding men and women in a joint collaboration. This rare combination of business executives, professional consultants, successful authors, and leadership scholars has come together with a common theme: new times call for new leadership.

Competitive Business, Caring Business
Daryl S. Paulson, Ph.D. $14.95/£12.50
This book provides managers and executives with new tools for finding personal satisfaction in their professional contributions. Daryl Paulson, the CEO of BioScience Laboratories, Inc., demonstrates the true meaning of "integral business." He shows how the work of human science theorist Ken Wilber applies to business, and explains why the process of "doing business" must be considered in a holistic and integral manner.

Because People Matter   Jurriaan Kamp $12.95/£9.99
The co-founder of *Ode* magazine argues that the world economy is not only based on money, but also on human choices. He offers insights on a new method of dealing with national income; taxing the use of raw materials rather than income; a world trade based on reciprocity; money without interest; and the liability of shareholders and managers for negligence and environmental damage.

PARAVIEW PRESS and PARAVIEW SPECIAL EDITIONS

use digital print-on-demand technology (POD), a revolution in publishing that makes it possible to produce books without the massive printing, shipping, and warehousing costs that traditional publishers incur. For more information, please visit our website at www.paraview.com, where you can also sign up for *Conscious Planet,* Paraview's free monthly media guide.

www.ingramcontent.com/pod-product-compliance
Lightning Source LLC
Chambersburg PA
CBHW031214270326
41931CB00006B/561